Let's Have Fun Teaching English
—From Theory to Practice—

ここから始めよう児童英語！
―理論から実践へ―

小原弥生
豊田典子
髙橋まり
Steven Rogers

NAN'UN-DO

Let's Have Fun Teaching English
From Theory to Practice

Copyright © 2019
by

Yayoi Obara
Noriko Toyoda
Mari Takahashi
Steven Rogers

All rights Reserved.

No part of this book may be reproduced in any form without written permission from the authors and Nan'un-do Co., Ltd.

このテキストの音声を無料で視聴（ストリーミング）・ダウンロードできます。自習用音声としてご活用ください。
以下のサイトにアクセスしてテキスト番号で検索してください。

https://nanun-do.com　テキスト番号 [512005]

※ 無線 LAN（WiFi）に接続してのご利用を推奨いたします。
※ 音声ダウンロードは Zip ファイルでの提供になります。
　お使いの機器によっては別途ソフトウェア（アプリケーション）の導入が必要となります。

※ Let's Have Fun Teaching English 音声ダウンロードページは以下の QR コードからもご利用になれます。

はしがき

　本書は，子どもに英語を教えることを目指す大学生，短大生，専門学校の学生のための総合英語教科書です。さらに，現役の幼稚園教員，小学校教員，中学校教員，児童英語指導者，英語教育に興味を持つ方々も使用できる内容です。また，現職教員のスキルアップ研修用テキストとしても使用できますので，活用していただければ幸いです。(尚，本書では外国語を「英語」とします。)

　小学校の外国語活動の歴史を振り返ると2011年に第5，6学年で必須となりました。そして，2020年度からは高学年（第5，6年生）が教科型となり，中学年（第3，4学年）は外国語活動として必修となっています。高学年では「聞く」「話す」に加え，「読む」「書く」指導が行われ，ますます，英語の内容や指導方法も高度になってきています。単に英語の知識や指導力のみだけでなく，第二言語習得の知識も必要とされてくるでしょう。また，保護者の英語教育に対する関心も非常に高まっていますので，教員になると様々な理論を準備しておき，質問や疑問に対して理論で答えることも必要となってきます。

　このような状況下では，教員は従来の「歌って，踊って，ゲームをして」ではなく，外国語科，外国語活動の目的や目標，指導内容や方法，評価方法などをしっかりと身につけておくことが肝要です。また，英語の指導力と専門性の向上が一層求められています。そのため，この総合的な指導に応えられるような役割を担う教科書が必要だと考えました。

　児童の発達段階や集中度などを鑑みると，中学校の英語教育の前倒しの形で教えていくのは難しいでしょう。そこで児童英語の指導法を学び，学生自身の英語の能力を高める学生用教科書が必要とされています。さらには言語教育の理論と専門的な英語の技能とともに，指導技術も要求されます。本書はこれらを踏まえ，理論とClassroom Englishに加えて，学生自身の英語力を高めることができる教科書を目指しました。児童英語教育界のニーズに答えた一冊になってくれることを願ってやみません。

　私たち著者は，全員小学校教員の経験があり，実際に大学の現場で小学校教員養成課程に在籍している学生の英語の授業を担当してきました。小学校教員の多忙さは実際に経験してきましたが，現状でも常にそのことは指摘されています。是非，学生のうちに研鑽を積み，現場では基礎知識をもとに実際に児童に出会って刺激を受けながら改善し，発展してほしいと考えます。

本書の特徴

1. 児童英語教育に関する基本的知識・理論，指導技術を学ぶことができます。
2. 聴解力，コミュニケーション能力，読解力，作文力が身につく活動が各レッスンに含まれています。
3. 実際にクラスで使える活動やClassroom Englishが学べます。
4. 確認問題でそのレッスンの理解度が測定できます。

本書の構成

◆ 理論

　英語教育に関する基礎的な理論を身につけます。児童に英語を教える際に学んでおくべき理論が，各レッスンのテーマごとに日本語で書かれています。本書では，児童教育に携わる方にとって必須の学習指導要領，英語教授法，第二言語習得論，4技能，考える力，学習活動，評価と模擬授業などを扱います。

◆ Let's Talk

　レッスンテーマに対する導入の英会話です。学級担任とALT（外国語指導助手）が授業の打ち合わせや準備をする際の会話，授業内で児童たちと話す際の会話，授業の導入などがあります。Let's Talk と Conversation は個別の内容としているレッスンもありますが，授業の導入や発展といった課もあり，バリエーション豊かな設定となっています。

◆ Conversation

　様々な会話から聴解力と発信力をつけます。まず，会話を読んで空欄に入れる語を予測します。次にCDを聴いて，空欄に適語を入れ聴解力を養いましょう。その後，パートナーと role play reading（役割読み）をします。ここで overlapping（同時読み），pair shadowing（ペアでの影読み），read and look up（顔あげ読み）などの様々な音読の手法を取り入れながら，最終的に暗唱できるように頑張りましょう。また，学生が独自で文を変えて読むなどバリエーションをつけ，オリジナルの会話を作ることによって発信力をつけることにつながります。内容は授業内で使用される会話やゲーム，教員間の会話です。

◆ Let's Read

　読解力と専門知識の獲得を目的にしています。各レッスンのテーマに関する理論やその内容を幅広く深めていくための英文です。長文内容を理解したかどうか確認する問題として，選択肢の中から正解を選ぶ形式の3つの設問があります。選択肢を選ぶだけでなく，その根拠を示す文を指摘する問題もあります。それによって，確実にその内容が把握できているかがわかります。行がまたがっている場合は，その文の始まっている行数と終わっている行数を書くようにしましょう。

◆ 知っておこう！キーワード

　レッスンのテーマやその関連する話題につながる主な単語を5つ挙げました。さらなる知識の修得のために，役立てましょう。

◆ 確認問題

　レッスン全体の確認です。Let's Talk, Conversation, Let's Read の内容を理解した上で，さらに英語力を深める問題となります。整序作文問題や，指定された語を使い英文を作成する問題，さらに日本語をもとに英文を書く問題があり，平易な問題から難度の高い問題へと推移する流れになっています。

尚，各担当は以下のとおりです。

小原弥生　はしがき，　Lesson 4,　Lesson 5,　Lesson 6,　Lesson 7,　Lesson 8
豊田典子　Lesson 1,　Lesson 2,　Lesson 3,　Lesson12,　Lesson 13,　Lesson 15
高橋まり　Lesson 9,　Lesson 10,　Lesson 11,　Lesson 14
Steven Rogers 英文の Proof Reading, 他

　最後に，本書の出版にあたっては，多くの方々にお世話になりました。とりわけ，（株）南雲堂の丸小雅臣氏には多くの励ましと企画，編集，校正など助言とご支援をいただきました。伊藤宏実氏には，校正段階で大変丁寧なご支援をいただきました。その他（株）南雲堂の皆様方にも大変お世話になりました。ここに感謝の意を述べさせていただきます。

著者一同

Table of Contents

Part 1　小学校英語を取り巻く状況

| Lesson 1 | An Overview of the Courses of Study | 10 |

学習指導要領を考える — 小中連携を視野に入れて

| Lesson 2 | English Teaching Methodologies (1) | 14 |

主要な英語教授法の変遷を概観する — 言語習得理論を踏まえて

| Lesson 3 | English Teaching Methodologies (2) | 18 |

小学校英語の指導法 — 楽しく効果的に

Part 2　指導者と指導内容

| Lesson 4 | Teachers | 24 |

小学校英語の指導者 — 効果的なティーム・ティーチング

| Lesson 5 | Teaching Listening | 28 |

リスニングの指導法—英語リズムの体得

| Lesson 6 | Teaching Speaking | 32 |

スピーキングの指導法 —「やり取り」「発表」「ストーリーテリング」

| Lesson 7 | Teaching Reading | 36 |

リーディングの指導法 — 文字の識別・読解

| Lesson 8 | Teaching Writing | 40 |

ライティングの指導法 — 大文字・小文字，語句や表現

目　次

Part 3　活動・教材・教具

Lesson 9　**Activities to Get Children Involved (1)**　46
リズム・メロディを通した活動 ― 歌・チャンツを用いて

Lesson 10　**Activities to Get Children Involved (2)**　50
知的好奇心を刺激する活動 ― ゲーム・クイズ を用いて

Lesson 11　**Activities to Get Children Involved (3)**　54
デジタル教材を活かした活動 ― ICT・映像を用いて

Lesson 12　**Developing Children's Thinking Skills (1)**　58
考えさせる指導法（1）― 自発的に学び，考える力を育む

Lesson 13　**Developing Children's Thinking Skills (2)**　62
考えさせる指導法（2）― より豊かな思考力を目指して

Part 4　評価と模擬授業

Lesson 14　**Evaluation**　68
評価を考える ― CAN-DO リストの活用

Lesson 15　**Teaching Practice**　72
模擬授業 ― 指導案作成から授業実践まで

Part 1　小学校英語を取り巻く状況

Lesson 1

An Overview of the Courses of Study

学習指導要領を考える ― 小中連携を視野に入れて

2008年度の学習指導要領改訂により，「外国語活動」は小学校第5，6学年に新設されました。その後，移行期間を経て，2011年度からは年間35単位時間の必修科目となりました。2020年度施行の学習指導要領では，「外国語活動」は第3，4学年の必修科目となり，第5，6学年には「外国語科」という教科が新設されました。一般的に，「小学校英語」と呼ばれている授業は，指導要領における「外国語活動」「外国語科」の中で，英語を中心とした外国語に関する活動や教科ということになります。

このような英語教育の早期化は，日本の英語教育に，または，日本人の英語力にどのような影響をもたらすのでしょうか。学習指導要領（2020年度）における主なポイントは以下になります。

	外国語活動	外国語科
履修義務	必修	必修教科
学年	中学年	高学年
学習時間	年間35単位時間（週1回程度）	年間70単位時間（週2回程度）
教科書	学校・教員による採択	文部科学省検定済教書
評価	文章による評価	数値化による評価
目標	・コミュニケーションを図る素地となる資質・能力の育成 ・幅広い言語に関する能力の育成 ・外国語の音声や基本的な表現へ慣れ親しむこと	・コミュニケーションを図る基礎となる資質・能力の育成 ・「聞く」「話す」「読む」「書く」の4技能の育成 ・音声から文字への指導 ・言語活動を通した，文や文構造への理解 ・小中の連携

中学年では，「聞く」「話す」と言った音声面を中心としたコミュニケーションを通して，英語に慣れ親しみます。高学年では，それを基礎として，中学校外国語へのつながりにも配慮された多くの活動を通して，英語を学んでいきます。例えば，英語の文字や単語などの認識，日本語と英語の音声，文構造，語順などの違いやそれぞれの特徴への気づきなどを促すことが指導者に求められます。このような段階的な活動を経て，中学校へのスムーズな連携となるような配慮がされています。

多様な言語活動を通して，児童が気持ちや考えを表現できるようになるためには，自ら思考，判断，表現する授業作りが重要です。外国語教育を取り巻く学習環境の中で，小学校で英語を教えることの意義や目的を考え，そのために知識や理解を深めていきましょう。

Part 1

> コミュニケーションの活動の前にウォーミングアップをすることで，授業の始まりを円滑にし，また最後のまとめをすることで，学習事項の定着を図ることができます。

Let's Talk

T1: Good morning, Mr. Chris!
T2: Good morning. How are you today?
T1: Good, and you?
T2: I feel great. By the way, can you call me "Chris" or "Mr. White"?
T1: Sure, Chris.
T2: That's better. Thank you!

Conversation

Listen to the dialogue and fill in the blanks, then role play the conversation.
会話文を聞いて，空欄に適語を入れなさい。その後，パートナーと会話をしましょう。

───── 〈Greeting〉 ─────

T: Hello, everyone. 1._____ are you today?

Ss: Great, thank you.

T: Now, I'm going to take 2._____. Please 3._____ your hand and say, "4._____." Masako.

S: 4._____!

───── 〈Warming up〉 ─────

T: What day of the 5._____ is it today?

S: 6._____ Monday.

T: That's 7._____. Great! OK, let's get 8._____!

───── 〈Consolidation at the end of the lesson〉 ─────

T: That's all for today. You all 9._____ hard today. Did you have a good 10._____?

Ss: Yes!

T: Very good! Goodbye, everyone. See you next week.

Let's Read

Read the passage and answer the questions.
文を読んで次の質問に答えましょう。答えの根拠となる文の行数を（　）に書きましょう。

　Hi, I'm Haruto Tanaka, a homeroom teacher of the third grade of Nansei Elementary School in Yokohama.

　Today, let me talk about an English lesson I gave at my school. Honestly speaking, I was a little bit nervous. It was the first time for most students to study English at school. Afterwards, I found all of the students enjoyed the lesson, and I feel better now. I'm going to talk about how it went. 5

　Our class uses "Let's Speak Together 1," a textbook that is compliant with the latest Courses of Study. First, I showed a video so that my students could watch and think about the people and the languages in the world. Some students noticed the Korean greeting, and most could say "hello." One student stated that "jumbo" was a Swahili greeting. Many 10 students did not know countries' names in English, so it was fun for them to learn the names.

　After watching the video, I asked them a few questions in English, such as the number of countries in the world, and which language was spoken in which country. I prepared everything on digital slides so they could simply raise their hands to choose answers. Finally, we had a small discussion in Japanese about the world. I wasn't sure if we should 15 keep on speaking in English, but I decided to use Japanese to encourage all my students to say what they thought. Overall, it was a good lesson for the students to learn about the world and world languages. They are now looking forward to the next English lesson.

　There are many opinions about how and when to teach English in elementary schools, and I am still not sure which way is the best. I believe that we should continue 20 seeking the best for students so that they can communicate and think globally.　(307 words)

1. *Why was Mr. Tanaka nervous?* （根拠___行目）
   a. Because it was his first time at school
   b. Because he had never taught English at the school
   c. Because most of the students had never studied English at school
2. *What was not likely included in his English class?* （根拠___行目）
   a. Korean language　b. English greetings　c. Writing the alphabet in English
3. *Which language (s) does he think teachers should use in class?* （根拠___行目）
   a. English and Japanese　b. English only　c. Not sure

知っておこう！キーワード | *Choose the correct answer.* 次の語の意味をa〜eの中から選びましょう。

1. compliant with (　)　2. the Courses of Study (　)
3. the third grade of elementary school (　)　4. homeroom teacher (　)
5. Ministry of Education, Culture, Sports, Science and Technology of Japan (MEXT) (　)
a. 学習指導要領　b. 準拠している　c. 小学３年生　d. 学級担任　e. 文部科学省

Part 1

> **EXERCISES** 確認問題
> 1. *Complete the sentences according to the directions.* 指示に従って文を完成しましょう。
> 2. *After checking your answers, practice reading the correct sentences aloud.*
> 答え合わせをしたら，正しい文を音読しましょう。

❶ *Make English sentences using the words below.* T05
日本文を読み，英語の語句を並びかえてください。（文頭は大文字ではありません）

1. では，出席を取ります。
 (I'm / attendance / going / to / take / now).

    _____

2. 始めましょう。
 (get / started / let's).

    _____

3. 手を挙げて「はい」と言ってください。
 (your / "Here" / raise / say / please / hand / and /,).

    _____

4. 私は 3 年の担任です。
 (grade / the / homeroom / of / I'm / a / teacher / third).

    _____

5. 今日，私は学校で英語の授業をしました。(There is one word missing. 1 語を補ってください。)
 (English / today / gave / lesson / I / school / an / ,).

    _____

❷ *Translate the Japanese sentences into English.* T06
日本文を読み，本文を参考にして英文を書いてください。

1. 今日は何曜日ですか？ (Use "week.")

    _____

2. 私のことを「クリス」と呼んでくれますか？

    _____

3. すべての児童が授業を楽しみました。
 All of the _____

4. 今日の授業は以上です。

    _____

5. みんな，よく頑張りました。

    _____

An Overview of the Courses of Study   13

Lesson 2

English Teaching Methodologies (1)

主要な英語教授法の変遷を概観する ― 言語習得理論を踏まえて

　児童の関心を引きつけ，モチベーションを上げ，効果的に英語を身につけてもらうためには，どのような教え方をすればよいのでしょうか。様々な教授法，児童の発達していく認知段階や，言葉の習得などを研究し，多様な観点から理解していく必要があります。外国語教授法は今日に至るまで様々な変遷を遂げていますが，過去の教授法を比較検討し，それぞれの長所短所を理解しておくことは有益です。

　「文法訳読法」は多くの国で実践されてきました。19世紀には，目標言語だけで指導を行う「直接法」が注目を浴び，日本でも1920年代にパーマー（H. E. Palmer）が招かれ，聞き取り・会話練習から始める「オーラル・メソッド」が開発され，普及が図られました。

　1960年代には，構造言語学や行動主義心理学に基づいた「オーディオリンガル・メソッド」がアメリカで流行しました。これは，文型などの反復練習（パターン・プラクティス）を多用したメソッドで，耳から入ってくる音を重視し，その言葉が口をついて出るまで繰り返すという学習法です。この練習法では正確性は向上しますが，コミュニケーション上の意思伝達ができるようになるのは難しいと言えます。また，心理学者アッシャー（J. Asher）によって，言語活動と全身動作を連合させる「全身反応法」が提唱されました。

　1970年代に入ると，コミュニケーションやお互いをわかり合い，尊重し合うことを目標とした言語学習という概念も現れ始め，コミュニカティブ・アプローチ（コミュニケーション能力を重視した言語学習観）の一つである「概念・機能シラバス」や，欧州評議会による実際の言語使用を中心とした教授計画（シラバス）が提唱されました。さらに，人間主義的教育をベースに，外国語教育は単に外国の言葉だけを教えるのではなく，「コミュニティ・ランゲージ・ラーニング（CLL）」のような全人格的成長を促すものと捉える教授法も提唱され，学習者中心の学びが盛んに謳われるようになりました。

　1980年代になると，より多くの研究がなされ，様々な教授法が考案されました。クラッシェン（S. Krashen）は第二言語習得に関する5つの仮説を発表し，それをきっかけに，アウトプットやインタラクションの重要性にも配慮した多様なアプローチ，教授法が提唱されました。他にも，学習者のニーズに基づいてタスクを選定し，タスクを中心にシラバスを編成する「タスク中心教授法」など，より実践的な教授法も編み出されました。

　どのような教授法も指導者の英語力や指導技術が問われます。理論的には素晴らしいものでも，指導者の負担が大きすぎる場合や，学習者に適していない場合は普及しないこともあります。教授法を選ぶ際には，配慮すべき多くの点があります。

Part 1

授業中，児童への指示は目標言語である英語で行うことが望ましいとされています。指示を聞いて体を動かすことそのものがコミュニケーションであり，英語を自然に身につける機会になります。

Let's Talk

T07
S05

T1: Hi, Chris. Shall we play a color game today with the third graders, as they learned the names of colors last week?

T2: That's a great idea. That will make it interactive.

T1: Yes. They should communicate with each other more.

T2: I agree. They can practice the question "What color is this?"

Conversation

T08
S06

Listen to the dialogue and fill in the blanks, then role play the conversation.
会話文を聞いて，空欄に適語を入れなさい。その後，パートナーと会話をしましょう。

T: Today, let's 1._____ a color game. Does anybody know 2._____ to play it? Now, I'll 3._____ you how to play the game. Look at these cards. What 4._____ are they?

Ss: Red. Blue. Yellow. Green.

T: Good job! OK, now, everybody, 5._____ up a card one 6._____ one from the box, then 7._____ back to your seats. Don't show the card to 8._____ else!

─〈All pick up cards.〉─

T: Do you 9._____ a color card? Now, Keita, please come to the front and say, "What color is this?" Don't show it to the others!

S1: What color is this?

S2: Red!

S1: No! What color is this?

S3: Yellow!

S1: Yes!

T: Great job! Now 10._____ a pair and ask each other!

Let's Read

Read the passage and answer the questions.
文を読んで次の質問に答えましょう。答えの根拠となる文の行数を（ ）に書きましょう。

We had a parent-teacher meeting today, and there were a few questions about our English education policy in this elementary school. I found that most parents were concerned about when to start, how to teach, and who should teach English class. A mother from my homeroom class asked me whether her child was doing fine. She said her son could not translate a simple word such as "an apple" or "a monkey" at home. A 5 senior teacher in charge of English education explained the "direct method." He said, "We don't use Japanese during the lessons. Our students learn English without translation so that they can acquire English more naturally." He also talked about the stages of psychological development, known as "the silent period." This is the period of time when children stay quiet before starting to talk. This motivated other parents with 10 further questions. One showed his concern for his daughter, who did not want to go to school because of English class. I promised him to talk to her personally, while referring to Krashen's "affective filter hypothesis."

This kind of knowledge can be a powerful tool to persuade parents. The theory that attracted parents most was the "critical period hypothesis," which claims there are 15 limitations of age to learn a language. I added that there are many academic research papers that suggest that a late start in language learning does not have a negative effect, and in some cases has a positive effect.

(244 words)

silent period（沈黙期）言語習得の初期段階にリスニング理解を主にし、発話があまり見られない段階。
affective filter hypothesis（情意フィルター仮説）Krashen（1982）が提唱したモニターモデルの5つの仮説の1つ。情意的要因が第二言語習得にどのように関わるのかを説明しようとする仮説。不安の少ない学習者ほど習得が促されるとする。

1. *Who do you think likely wrote this passage?*（根拠＿＿行目）
    a. A principal of an elementary school
    b. A parent
    c. A teacher
2. *Which question will a parent likely ask during the meeting?*（根拠 行目）
    a. Are you taking students to a foreign country?
    b. Who is teaching English at school?
    c. Will you teach French at school?
3. *Is it important to learn knowledge of language acquisition?*（根拠＿＿行目）
    a. Yes, it is not important to persuade parents.
    b. Yes, it could be a powerful tool to persuade parents.
    c. No, it is a waste of time to persuade parents.

知っておこう！キーワード | *Choose the correct answer.* 次の語の意味をa〜eの中から選びましょう。

1. theory （ ）　　2. hypothesis （ ）　　3. parent teacher association （ ）
4. direct method （ ）　　5. grammar translation method （ ）
a. 直接法　　b. 文法訳読法　　c. 理論　　d. 仮説　　e. PTA

Part 1

> **EXERCISES** 確認問題
> 1. **Complete the sentences according to the directions.** 指示に従って文を完成しましょう。
> 2. **After checking your answers, practice reading the correct sentences aloud.**
> 答え合わせをしたら，正しい文を音読しましょう。

❶ *Make English sentences using the words below.*
日本文を読み，英語の語句を並びかえてください。（文頭は大文字ではありません）　　T10

1. 色のゲーム（「カラーゲーム」）をしましょう。
(color / let's / play / game / a)!
_____

2. 自分の席に戻りなさい。
(back / your / to / go / seats).
_____

3. そのやり方を知っている人はいますか？
(it / know / how / anybody / to / play / does)?
_____

4. それらはどんな色ですか？
(are / colors / what / they)?
_____

5. ほとんどの親がいつ英語学習を始めるべきか心配していました。
(There is one word missing. 1語を補ってください。)
(were / class / start / English / about / to / parents / when / most).
_____

❷ *Translate the Japanese sentences into English.*
日本文を読み，本文を参考にして英文を書いてください。　　T11

1. 一人ずつ箱からカードを一枚引いて。
Pick up a _____

2. 私がみなさんにゲームのやり方を見せましょう。(Use "show.")
_____

3. 二人一組になってお互いに尋ねあってください。(Use "pair.")
_____

4. 前に出てきて「これは何色ですか」と言ってください。
_____

5. 私は，児童と個人的に話すことを，彼に約束しました。(Use "personally.")
_____

English Teaching Methodologies (1)   17

Lesson 3

English Teaching Methodologies (2)

小学校英語の指導法 ― 楽しく効果的に

　日本の英語教育では，文法に基づいて，英文を正確に日本語に訳していく「文法訳読法」が多く用いられてきました。しかし，昨今では，コミュニケーションを重視した外国語教授法が着目され，多くの指導法が実践されています。特に，小学校における外国語活動や外国語科では，デジタル教材，音楽，リズム，カードなどを利用した様々な指導が行われています。また，外国語学習を通して，考える力や国際理解を深めることも目的としているため，英語の習得にとどまらず，国内外の動向にも関心を持ってもらえるよう，レッスン内容を工夫する必要があります。

　外国語を教える際に，その外国語で教えるのか，母語で教えるのかという点は，長らく議論されてきた問題です。中学・高校の英語の授業では，特に文法説明などは日本語でなされてきたのではないかと思います。現在では，英語は英語で教えるという「直接法」による授業が推奨されています。直接法は，学習者の年齢が低いほど親和性が高いため，小学校英語教育の中でも積極的に取り入れられれば理想的です。

　以下の表には，小学校英語の指導に多く用いられる活動と，児童の「聴解」「発話」「交流」「文化などへの気づき」のどれに主な影響をもたらすのか，どの要素を活性化させるのか，の目安を示しています。いずれの活動も相互に関連性があります。

指導法・活動	内容	活動の主なねらい			
		聴解	発話	交流	気づき
視聴覚教材, リスニング	英語の聞き取りや内容理解の練習に利用したり，視聴を通して文化などへの児童の気づきを促す。	○		○	○
全身反応法 (TPR)	英語の指示に対してすぐに動作で反応することで，英語の自然なインプットを促す。聞き取った英語に反応して自然に行動させ，児童に「できた」という達成感をもたせる。	○			
歌，チャンツ，ジングル	リズムをつけて繰り返し口ずさむ活動。発音，強弱，リズムを身につけ，表現を覚える際に有効。聞き取らせたり，ジェスチャーをつけたり，単語を入れ替えさせるなどのアクティビティに応用できる。	○	○		
ロールプレイ	ごっこ遊びのように，役割を決めてペアやグループワークをする。ものの売り買い，機内での乗務員とのやりとり，道を尋ねるなど，シチュエーションベースの会話の練習が可能。劇のセリフのような暗記にならないよう，自分の言葉で発話できるように，単語を入れ替えさせるなどの工夫が必要である。	△	○	○	
インタビュー	児童同士での自発的なコミュニケーションを促す。練習した表現を使って，自分の聞きたいことを尋ね，伝えたいことを発話する実践的な活動。質問を考えることで文化の違いへの気づきにも発展させることができる。	△	○	○	○
読み聞かせ, リーディング	絵本の読み聞かせを通した，読むことに慣れるための活動。まとまった文章を聞いて理解できるようになったら，自分で読めるような指導につなげる。文章の内容を通じて思考力を養う活動にも応用ができる。	○			○

Part 1

英語でアクティビティの説明をする際は，二人の教師でデモンストレーションをすることで，児童は興味を持って説明を見聞きすることができます。

Let's Talk

T1: I'm thinking of playing Go Fish. How can we explain the game?
T2: We can give a demonstration. Let's show the students how to play.
T1: Great. How can we start?
T2: We say, "Watch us!" with gestures to get students' attention.
T1: I see, then?
T2: And then, we show how to play, speaking slowly.

Conversation

Listen to the dialogue and fill in the blanks, then role play the conversation.
会話文を聞いて，空欄に適語を入れなさい。その後，パートナーと会話をしましょう。

T1: We'll show you how to play Go Fish. I have three 1._____ of alphabet cards. 2._____ us. 3._____ the cards. Give five cards 4._____. I'll put the 5._____ of the cards here. We call it a pool. Now look at your cards. Do you have a "K"?

T2: No, I 6._____. Go fish!

〈T1 has to pick up a card from the pool.〉

T1: I have a 7._____ of "K"s.

T2: Do you have an "F"?

T1: Yes! Here you 8._____.

T2: Thank you. I have a pair of "F"s.

T1: OK, everybody. Let's play the game! You have five minutes.

────〈After five minutes of playing Go Fish〉────

T1: 9._____ up! How 10._____ pairs do you have?

Ss: I have five pairs! I have six pairs!

T1: Oh, you are the winner!

Let's Read

Read the passage and answer the questions.
文を読んで次の質問に答えましょう。答えの根拠となる文の行数を（　）に書きましょう。

　Some criticize English classes where children play games and sing songs. However, teaching English to children is not the same as teaching adults. First of all, the vocabulary size of a child is quite limited compared to an adult. And their attention spans are short. For such learners, game-like activities can be used so that they can acquire English while having fun. As the child doesn't need an extensive English vocabulary, activities work well even with beginners. For example, drawing pictures can get students excited and interested in a variety of lessons.

　Last week I taught words for occupations and colors. Then, I asked the students to draw pictures of occupations they wanted to be. While they were drawing, I asked them "What do you want to be?" and "What color is this?" in English. After all the students had finished, they gave a presentation and enjoyed showing the pictures and saying occupations in English. With younger students, we can do the same activity with fruits or animals.

　I also use pattern practice with chants, songs, and jingles. They can easily copy teachers and remember the words. The important thing is to make these words cognitively usable by finding ways for students to use the vocabulary and phrases in the real world to deliver their own messages.

　Actually, I learned this from a mistake. I believed that the students had all learned everyday greetings, such as "How are you?," "I'm fine, thank you. And you?," after practicing every morning for two years. However, when a new ALT, Chris, asked them, "How are you doing?," they could not say even a word. This showed that the students could not use the phrases in a different situation or with other variations if they only learned with pattern practicing exercises. I learned a lot from that lesson and started to expose them to as many chances as possible to speak with their own words.

(321 words)

1. *Teaching English to adults is the same as teaching children. True or false?*　（根拠＿＿行目）
   a. True　　b. False　　c. Not mentioned above
2. *What is a good way to teach English to children?*　（根拠＿＿行目）
   a. Grammar　　b. Drawing pictures　　c. Limited vocabulary
3. *Why do you think the students could not answer Chris?*　（根拠＿＿行目）
   a. Because he spoke quietly
   b. Because he used a different phrase
   c. Because he did not smile at the students

知っておこう！キーワード　*Choose the correct answer.*　次の語の意味をa〜eの中から選びましょう。

1. activity (　)　　2. vocabulary (　)　　3. advanced student (　)
4. young student (　)　　5. attention span (　)
a. 児童生徒　　b. 語彙　　c. 活動　　d. 上級レベルの学習者　　e. 集中持続時間

Part 1

> **EXERCISES** 確認問題
> 1. Complete the sentences according to the directions. 指示に従って文を完成しましょう。
> 2. After checking your answers, practice reading the correct sentences aloud.
> 答え合わせをしたら，正しい文を音読しましょう。

❶ *Make English sentences using the words below.*   T15
日本文を読み，英語の語句を並びかえてください。(文頭は大文字ではありません)

1. Go Fish の仕方を説明します。
   (Go Fish / to / show / you / we'll / how / play)!
   _____

2. トランプを混ぜてください。
   (cards / the / shuffle).
   _____

3. 1人5枚ずつカードを配ってください。
   (give / cards / each / five).
   _____

4. "K" のカードのペアが揃いました。
   (pair / I / have / a / of / "K"s).
   _____

5. 残りのカードをここに置きます。(There is one word missing. 1語を補ってください。)
   (I'll / of / put / here / cards / the / the).
   _____

❷ *Translate the Japanese sentences into English.*   T16
日本文を読み，本文を参考にして英文を書いてください。

1. では，自分のカードを見てください。
   Now, look _____

2. あなたの勝ちです！(Use "winner.")
   _____

3. Go Fish をしようと思っています。(Use "thinking of.")
   _____

4. 先週，職業に関する言葉を教えました。(Use "career.")
   _____

5. アクティビティは初心者にも効果的です。(Use "work.")
   _____

English Teaching Methodologies (2)

Part 2 指導者と指導内容

Lesson 4

Teachers

小学校英語の指導者 ― 効果的なティーム・ティーチング

　小学校の外国語活動や外国語科においての指導者は，主に①学級担任（homeroom teacher, 以下 HRT），②外国語指導助手（assistant language teacher 以下 ALT），③非常勤講師（英語の堪能な外部講師），④地域ボランティア，⑤専科教員，⑥中学・高校の英語教師などです。ALT の配置状況は学校や自治体によっても違います。訪問回数が多い学校と少ない学校があります。また，必ずしも英語を母語とする ALT ばかりではありません。その場合，児童は彼らから，世界には英語母語話者の話す英語だけでなく多様な英語（Englishes）があり，現代は Englishes の時代だということを学ぶでしょう。

　さて，小学校で一番多く児童に接するのは HRT です。そして HRT は，他の教科の指導をすることはもちろん，英語も教えなくてはなりません。英語の知識や運用能力だけでなく英語を教える能力も必要とされます。また外国語という教科は，単に語学を教えるだけではありません。世界に存在する色々な言葉，色々な考え方を理解させることも求められています。いわゆる異文化理解教育です。学習指導要領にも「外国語の背景にある文化に対する理解を深め」とあります。他の言葉や文化を知ることは自分自身の言語や文化を振り返る機会を与えてくれます。それにより，自分の言語や文化を客観的に見ることができます。外国文化の背景を持つ ALT との授業は，このような多様性を教えるのに理想的です。

　この課ではみなさんと一緒にティーム・ティーチング（team teaching 以下 TT）をすることになる ALT との授業を考えてみましょう。（もちろん，TT は HRT と上記の③④⑤⑥の指導者とも行うことができます。）HRT は一人一人の児童の能力や性格もわかっていますので，個人を指名する時などは，HRT は ALT と打ち合わせをしておくとよいでしょう。また，ALT は言語運用能力に長けています。ティームを組み役割分担することによってそれぞれの良さがさらに増します。また，HRT と ALT とのコミュニケーションを見たり，聞いたりすることによって，児童は「先生はがんばって英語を使っている」と感じます。HRT が臆さずに ALT と会話することによって，良い学習者のロールモデルになることができます。このように児童をよく理解し能力も把握している HRT と，英語と英語を話す人々の文化についてよく理解している ALT との協力ですばらしい TT ができるでしょう。

　時間的に，また制度的に可能であれば，事前に指導案の検討や，授業で用意するものを打ち合わせておきましょう。例えば，ALT の出身地を児童に説明する際に必要な地図，写真，動画などは持参してもらうか，HRT が用意しておくことで，安心して授業ができます。

Part 2

> ALTには，指導計画などで教員を助けるとともに，音声面，英語の使用法での手本となる役割があります。コミュニケーションを密にとって信頼関係を構築しましょう。

Let's Talk

HRT: Hello! Nice to meet you. My name is Sato Yumi. What's your name?
ALT: Nice to meet you, too. My name is Chris White.
HRT: Where are you from?
ALT: Melbourne, in Australia.
HRT: Interesting! How long have you been in Japan?
ALT: I just arrived a week ago.

Conversation

Listen to the dialogue and fill in the blanks, then role play the conversation.
会話文を聞いて，空欄に適語を入れなさい。その後，パートナーと会話をしましょう。

HRT: Is this your first 1._____ in Japan?

ALT: Yes. This is my first time.

HRT: What is your first 2._____ of Japan?

ALT: Everything is new for me. So I'm 3._____.

HRT: Have you ever 4._____ at an elementary school?

ALT: Yes, I have taught at a primary school in Australia.

HRT: What is a primary school?

ALT: It's the 5._____ as an elementary school.

HRT: I'm teaching fifth grade. You will teach them today. The classrooms for the fifth grade are on the second 6._____. All the classes are forty-five 7._____, and they have 8._____ thirty-five students. The first period 9._____ at eight forty. Please 10._____ free to ask me any questions.

Teachers 25

Let's Read

Read the passage and answer the questions.
文を読んで次の質問に答えましょう。答えの根拠となる文の行数を（　）に書きましょう。

　　Chris White came to Nansei Elementary School from Australia. Sato Yumi, the fifth-grade teacher, is in charge of foreign language education at her school. She asked Mr. White about his teaching experience at an elementary school. She learned that he had taught at a primary school in Australia. In his country, they call an elementary school a primary school. She found a new word for an elementary school. She was happy to hear ₅ that Mr. White had experience teaching at elementary school because it meant that he knew how to get along with young students.

　　She asked him about his former school in Australia. He explained that the young students had to be accompanied by their parents or family members to come to school and go back home until the students became third graders. It was new information for ₁₀ her. But of course, every country has its own way of doing things, she thought.

　　She asked him what brought him to Japan, and he answered that his former school had a sister school in Japan. Once, he welcomed the students and teachers from the Japanese sister school as guests in his school. He became interested in Japan, and he had wanted to come to Japan and teach children in Japan since then. Now his dream has ₁₅ come true.

(218 words)

1. *How did Sato Yumi feel when she welcomed Chris White as an ALT.?*
   （根拠　　行目）
   a. She was nervous because Chris didn't know anything about the students.
   b. She was happy to hear that Chris had experience teaching at a primary school.
   c. She was disappointed that Chris came from Australia.
2. *What do they call "shōgakkō" in Australia?* （根拠　　行目）
   a. Middle school　　b. Elementary school　　c. Primary school
3. *What brought Chris to Japan?* （根拠　　行目）
   a. The students from his sister school in Japan made him interested in Japan.
   b. He likes Japanese food.
   c. He didn't like his former school.

知っておこう！キーワード　| *Choose the correct answer.*　次の語の意味をa〜eの中から選びましょう。

1. ALT (　　)　　2. recess (　　)　　3. principal (　　)
4. school counselor (　　)　　5. school nurse (　　)
a. 養護教員　b. 休み時間　c. 校長　d. スクールカウンセラー　e. 外国語指導助手

Part 2

> **EXERCISES** 確認問題
> 1. *Complete the sentences according to the directions.* 指示に従って文を完成しましょう。
> 2. *After checking your answers, practice reading the correct sentences aloud.*
>   答え合わせをしたら、正しい文を音読しましょう。

❶ *Make English sentences using the words below.* 　　T20
日本文を読み、英語の語句を並びかえてください。（文頭は大文字ではありません）

1. あなたは日本にどれくらいいらっしゃいますか？
   (long / how / you / in / have / been /Japan)?
   _____

2. 日本に来るのは今回が初めてですか？
   (this / first / Japan / your / time / is / in)?
   _____

3. 日本の第一印象はいかがですか？
   (your / what / impression / is / Japan / of / first)?
   _____

4. 私は5年生を教えています。
   (teaching / I'm / grade / fifth).
   _____

5. あなたは小学校で教えたことがありますか？(There is one word missing. 1語を補ってください。)
   (you / ever / school / taught / an / have / elementary)?
   _____

❷ *Translate the Japanese sentences into English.* 　　T21
日本文を読み、本文を参考にして英文を書いてください。

1. 5年生の教室は2階にあります。
   The classrooms for _____

2. どんな質問でも、気軽に私に尋ねてください。(Use "free" and "feel.")
   _____

3. 1時間目は8時40分に始まります。
   _____

4. 私は小学校で教えた経験があります。(Use "elementary.")
   _____

5. すべての授業は45分間です。
   _____

Teachers 27

Lesson 5

Teaching Listening

> リスニングの指導法 ― 英語リズムの体得

　リスニングにおいて，学習者にとって困難なことの一つに，英語母語話者の話す速度についていけないということが挙げられます。日本語の場合，話すスピードは10秒間に15〜20文字程度，1分間に90〜120字といわれています。しかし，英語のスピードは10秒間に20〜25語程度，1分間に120〜150語話しているといわれています。

　もう一つの理由として，英語と日本語のリズムの違いがあります。日本語母語話者にとって英語の音声英語を体得するときに大事なことは，リズムだといわれています。日本語は音節がリズムを作るときに大事である（音節拍リズム，syllable-timed）のに対し，英語は強く言う音が中心となってリズムを作る（強勢拍リズム，stress-timed）ためです。

　強勢の置かれるものはどれかを見てみると下の例でいえば，1は dog, desk, Tom, fine, go であり，置かれないものは a, the, I'm, It's, I'll です。2では，house, myself, hear, go に強勢が置かれています。このようにリズムの基礎となる強く発音される度合の多いものは，名詞と動詞で，2番目に強く発音される度合の多いものは，形容詞，副詞だといわれています。また，疑問詞も強く発音されます。これらは内容語（名詞，動詞〈一般動詞〉，形容詞，副詞，指示代名詞，所有代名詞，疑問詞，再帰代名詞）といいます。相対的に機能語（人称代名詞，助動詞，前置詞，冠詞，接続詞，関係代名詞，Be 動詞）は聞こえにくくなります。

1. ・● 　 ・● 　 ・● 　 ・● 　 ・●
　　a dog 　 the desk 　 I'm Tom. 　 It's fine. 　 I'll go.
2. ・・● 　 ・・● 　 ・・● 　 ・・●
　　in the house 　 by myself 　 I can hear. 　 You must go.

　一つの単語でも日本語では1文字が1拍です。「ことぶき」は「タン，タン，タン，タン」の4拍です。street, strike は文字数が多くても1拍で発音されます。また，英語では音声変化を伴い，ある音がほとんど聞こえなくなったり（弱化），次の語と結びついたり（連結），なくなってしまう（脱落）こともあります。例えば，"want to" の 't' は2回発音されないのが一般的です。この点においても，「聴くこと」は，日本語と違い難しいということがわかります。そのため，多くの音源を聞かせて，自然な英語の音声に慣れ親しませることが大切です。また, HRT も十分に「聴くこと」の訓練を積むことが求められます。教師も試しに，わからなかった箇所を何度も英語母語話者と同じスピードで音読してみてください（overlapping）。自然に自分の読んだ言葉と同じ言葉を英語母語話者の述べた文の中から聞き取ることができるでしょう。児童にもそれを試してみましょう。きっと，「聞こえた！」という反応が返ってくると思います。このように英語のリズムを体得させることが必要です。

　最後に，「聴くこと」は，耳からだけでなく，考えることも重要だということです。聞きながら意味を考えたり，文法や文の構造を考えたりすれば，より正確な聴解力がつくことが期待できます。

Part 2

> 映画を見ていると母語話者同士の会話が聞き取れないことはありませんか？英語と日本語の話し方には根本的な違いがあるのです。児童にも会話文を聞かせて違いを理解させましょう。

Let's Talk

HRT: Phew!! It's difficult.
ALT: What?
HRT: It's hard for me to pick up the words in the movie. They speak too fast to catch each word.
ALT: Yes, English is different from Japanese. English is a stress-timed language while Japanese is syllable-timed. And there are some phonetic changes such as elision, linking, assimilation, and so on.

Conversation

Listen to the dialogue and fill in the blanks, then role play the conversation.
会話文を聞いて，空欄に適語を入れなさい。その後，パートナーと会話をしましょう。

HRT: Let's play the 1._____ am I game. This game is for listening practice. So you have to listen to Chris very carefully. Now, let's get started.
 Ss: Yes. OK.
ALT: Please listen to me very 2._____. I will give you some hints.
 S1: Gi-byu?
ALT: Yes, give you. I will give you some hints.
 S1: Ah, "give you."
ALT: I am a 3._____, and I live 4._____ the sea.
 S2: Ba-a-dan?
ALT: I am a bird, and I live 4._____ the sea.
 S3: Bird? Tori? Sea? Umi?
ALT: Yes.
 S3: Sea? Kamome?
 S4: Seagulls.
ALT: I **cannot** 5._____. I can not fly.
 Ss: Sea? Cannot fly? Oh, penguin! You are a penguin!
ALT: That's 6._____. I'm a penguin. Can you 7._____ us the quiz?
 S5: Yes, I can.
HRT: OK. Please.
 S5: I am an animal. I live in Australia. I like 8._____ trees. I eat 9._____ of *yūkari*. Who am I?
 Ss: Do you like *yūkari*? Are you a 10._____?
 S5: Yes, I am a 10._____!

※ユーカリ　eucalyptus

Let's Read

Read the passage and answer the questions.
文を読んで次の質問に答えましょう。答えの根拠となる文の行数を（　）に書きましょう。

　　Listening to English is very difficult for Japanese students because rhythms are very different. English is a stress-timed language while Japanese is syllable-timed. Also, the natural speech speed is faster than Japanese. This makes it difficult to catch every word in a sentence.

　　English also has a lot of phonetic changes. There are five main changes: they are 　5
1. contraction（短縮：I will→I'll）, 2. reduction（弱化：walking→walkin_g）, 3. deletion（脱落：good job→グッジョブ）, 4. linking（連結：turn on→ターノン）, and 5. assimilation（同化：miss you→ミシュー）. So it's hard for Japanese students to listen to English phrases or sentences.

　　Also, we as teachers have to help students notice that there are many consonants that 　10
are not followed by vowels in English. Since almost all consonants in Japanese are pronounced with vowels, students are apt to put a vowel after every consonant in English. Please have a look at the table below. A vowel always comes after a consonant in Japanese words, such as the 'r' and 'sh' in /arashi/. In English, however, /g/ in /dog/ is not followed by a vowel. This is one of the reasons Japanese learners cannot pick up 　15
English words. This Japanese pronunciation characteristic makes the number of syllables large in Japanese while the number of letters can be much shorter when written in kanji or Chinese characters. A good example is /kotobuki/, written as 寿.

	英語	日本語					
書記素	d, o, g	イヌ	犬	アラシ	嵐	コトブキ	寿
音素	/d/o/g	i/nu	i/nu	a/ra/shi	a/ra/shi	ko/to/bu/ki	ko/to/bu/ki
書記素数	3	2	1	3	1	4	1
音素数	3	2	2	3	3	4	4
拍数	1	2	2	3	3	4	4

　　So let students listen to a lot of English so they can get used to the sound and try to understand the meaning. A knowledge of grammar is also helpful. 　(252 words)　20

1. *What is different between English and Japanese rhythm?*（根拠＿行目）
   a. English is a stress-timed language while Japanese is syllable-timed.
   b. There is no difference between English and Japanese rhythm.
   c. English is a syllable-timed language while Japanese is stress-timed.
2. *Does Japanese have vowels in almost all syllables?*（根拠＿行目）
   a. Yes, it does.　　b. No, it doesn't.　　c. Yes, they are.
3. *What is important for the students to listen to in English?*（根拠＿行目）
   a. Having them listen to a lot of English and guess the meaning of the content.
   b. Without understanding the meaning, only listening is important.
   c. The students don't have to listen to English.

知っておこう！キーワード　*Choose the correct answer.*　次の語の意味をa〜eの中から選びましょう。

1. stress-timed（　　）　　2. deletion（　　）　　3. syllable-timed（　　）
4. reduction（　　）　　5. assimilation（　　）
a. 音節拍リズムの　　b. 強勢拍リズムの　　c. 脱落　　d. 同化　　e. 弱化

Part 2

EXERCISES 確認問題

1. *Complete the sentences according to the directions.* 指示に従って文を完成しましょう。
2. *After checking your answers, practice reading the correct sentences aloud.*
答え合わせをしたら，正しい文を音読しましょう。

❶ *Make English sentences using the words below.* T25
日本文を読み，英語の語句を並びかえてください。（文頭は大文字ではありません）

1. 彼らはあまりにも速く話しすぎる。
(speak / they / fast / too).

2. 私はそれぞれの単語が聞き取れない。
(catch / cannot / each / I / word).

3. 「私は誰でしょうゲーム」をしましょう。
(play / let's / who / game / am / I / the).

4. 私の言うことをよーく聞いてね。
(to / listen / carefully / me / very).

5. 私にとって映画に出てくる会話を理解するのは難しい。(There is one word missing. 1語を補ってください。)
It's (me / for / understand / hard / the / conversations) in the movie.

❷ *Translate the Japanese sentences into English.* T26
日本文を読み，本文を参考にして英文を書いてください。

1. いくつかヒントを出します。
I will give ＿＿＿＿＿＿＿＿＿＿

2. 私は海のそばに住んでいます。

3. あなたはクイズを出せますか？

4. 児童は，すべての子音の後に母音をつけがちです。

5. 文法の知識も役に立ちます。

Lesson 6

Teaching Speaking

スピーキングの指導法 ―「やりとり」「発表」「ストーリーテリング」

　2020年度施行の学習指導要領で注目されていることは，4技能の一つの「話すこと」が「話すこと［やり取り］」と「話すこと［発表］」に分かれて記載されていることです。話すことが二つに分かれて記載されているということは，「話すこと」が小中学校の英語教育に肝要であるということがうかがわれます。

　一般に，日本の英語教育ではアウトプットする機会が少ないといわれています。小学校で英語に初めて出会う場面からすぐに英語を使ってみるという体験は重要です。そのために，語彙，表現，音声に慣れさせましょう。年齢が上がるとともに上がるといわれているクラッシェン（S. Krashen）のいう情意フィルター（恥ずかしさなど）が中学生よりも低いので，積極的に話す児童が多いでしょう。

　まず，「話すこと［やり取り］」について説明します。［やり取り］とは，リスニングによってインプットされたものを理解し，それに対して答えや自分の考えをアウトプットすることです。この習慣をつけることにより，英語は日本語と同じようにキャッチボールしながら意思伝達をする一つの道具だということがわかるでしょう。ただ，それだけではなく，英語を使って相手を知り，隣人を知り，しいては外国の文化を知る。そして，自分の考えを発信し，自分を相手に理解してもらい，自分の文化を外国に発信するという言語観を小学校のうちから身につけることができます。

　次に，「話すこと［発表］」について述べます。これは，1対多数という場で，自分の考えや研究したことを発表し，英語で伝える能力を養います。英語母語話者の国では，Show and Tell を人前で発表する訓練だと位置づけ，就学以前から始めています。日本の小学校でも成果を上げています。その他，一分間スピーチ，プレゼンテーション，ペアでのスキットの発表，ストーリーテリングなど人前で述べる機会を多く与えましょう。中高生になるとディスカッションやディベートが考えられます。その素地を作るために話す機会を多く与えると良いでしょう。外国語活動や外国語科の時間だけではなく，他の教科でも慣れさせておくことが必要です。小学校の担任ならではのできることですが，他教科においても人前で自分の意見を発表させる機会を多く持たせるようにしましょう。

　［発表］において問われるのは正確さ（accuracy）と流暢さ（fluency）ですが，小学生の段階ではあまり，正確さにこだわらない方が良いように思われます。相手に自分のことを話し，相手からフィードバックをもらうなど，［やり取り］においては通じること（通じビリティ）が大切だと考えられます。また，話すことにおいて一番大事なことは話す内容です。最初は簡単な語や慣用句などを暗記させるのは大切ですが，児童がそれを習得した上で，考えたことを発話することはさらに大切です。そして，コミュニケーションの楽しさを体験させ，達成感を味わわせましょう。英語の技能として，「聴くこと」，「話すこと［発表］」，「話すこと［やり取り］」，「読むこと」，「書くこと」だけでなく，「考えること」が加われば，鬼に金棒です。

Part 2

スピーキングの力をつけるにはどのような活動が効果的でしょうか。中でも Show and Tell の活動が一つの良い例ではないでしょうか。話すことにおける［発表］と生徒間の［やり取り］の両方をこの活動で獲得できます。自信をもって行わせるようにしましょう。

Let's Talk

HRT: I would like my students to speak in English class. Do you have any good ideas?

ALT: What about using a lot of group work or pair work? The students can consult each other and talk a lot in pairs or groups so that they feel relaxed.

HRT: That's a good idea! What are we going to do for the next lesson?

ALT: What about Show and Tell in the groups and then in front of the class?

HRT: OK. Other students can see the realia. So they will be interested in the speech, too. It's interesting. Let's try!

Conversation

Listen to the dialogue and fill in the blanks, then role play the conversation.
会話文を聞いて、空欄に適語を入れなさい。その後、パートナーと会話をしましょう。

HRT: Let's do Show and Tell next week.

S1: What is Show and Tell?

HRT: It is a way to 1._____ public speaking and 2._____ skills in the classroom.

S1: And?

HRT: You can 3._____ anything to school.

Ss: Toys. OK? Food. OK?

HRT: Yes. Anything is OK. You can bring your 4._____.

S2: What is a treasure?

HRT: Do you know Treasure 5._____?

S3: Shima.

HRT: Yes, what is a treasure?

Ss: Takara. Takaramono.

HRT: Right. And you will 6._____ it. In 7._____ words, you will talk about it.

S4: In English?

HRT: Of 8._____. And other students will ask you some questions about the 9._____. OK?

S5: 10._____ interesting.

Teaching Speaking 33

Let's Read

Read the passage and answer the questions.
文を読んで次の質問に答えましょう。答えの根拠となる文の行数を（ ）に書きましょう。

There are a lot of ways for students to develop their speaking skills. One good way is Show and Tell, a school activity in which a child brings an object to class and tells the other children about it. Students can bring anything from home to the classroom.

When I was in the seventh grade, I brought my carrier pigeon to the classroom. It is said the pigeon can fly back home from places as far as 1,000 km away. People used to use pigeons to send messages in olden times. They would attach a letter to one of the pigeon's legs and release it. There are even pigeon races. One of them is the 1,000 km race. The possibility of the pigeon returning home is 10 percent.

I talked about my pigeon, about how old he was, how I loved him, and how I took part in the 200 km race while showing him to the other students. There were many questions from my friends. "How long have you kept the pigeon?," "What's his name?," "Can you tell me about the race?," "How long did it take for him to fly back?," "Why do you like the pigeon?," "Why did you begin to keep it?" and so on. I could answer with confidence because I loved that pigeon and knew him very well. After Show and Tell was over, I let him fly from the window of the classroom to my house. Everyone gave me a big hand. It was fun.

If you have something you are very interested in and love very much, you will be eager to put a lot of effort into your presentation, and this may lower your affective filter. You will study about your topic and how to say what you want to say in English. It can motivate you to study English, too. Then the other students will know you well. You will become closer.

(322 words)

1. *What did the speaker show and tell?* （根拠___行目）
   a. A carrier bag   b. A carrier pigeon   c. His career
2. *Why was he able to answer the questions from the other students?* （根拠___行目）
   a. Because his pronunciation was good
   b. Because his teacher taught him how to answer
   c. Because he loved that pigeon and knew him very well
3. *When you talk about things you like, your affective filter may …* （根拠___行目）
   a. go down.   b. go up.   c. be the same as before.

知っておこう! キーワード | *Choose the correct answer.* 次の語の意味をa〜eの中から選びましょう。

1. consult (　)   2. precious (　)   3. opinion (　)   4. treasure (　)
5. recitation (　)
a. 宝   b. 意見   c. 相談する   d. 大切な   e. 暗記・暗唱

Part 2

> **EXERCISES** 確認問題
> 1. *Complete the sentences according to the directions.* 指示に従って文を完成しましょう。
> 2. *After checking your answers, practice reading the correct sentences aloud.*
> 答え合わせをしたら，正しい文を音読しましょう。

❶ *Make English sentences using the words below.*
日本文を読み，英語の語句を並びかえてください。（文頭は大文字ではありません）

1. ショーアンドテルは人前で話す練習のための一方法です。
(practice / way / to / Show and Tell / public / a / is / speaking).

2. あなたは学校に何を持ってきてもよいです。
(you / anything / bring / can / school / to).

3. 他の児童はスピーチに興味を持つでしょう。
(students / other / be / interested / in / will / speech / the).

4. 私は，教室に私の伝書バトを持って行きました。
(brought / carrier / my / pigeon / the / to / classroom / I).

5. それは英語を学ぶための動機になります。(There is one word missing. 1語を補ってください。)
(can / it / to / you / English / study).

❷ *Translate the Japanese sentences into English.*
日本文を読み，本文を参考にして英文を書いてください。

1. 伝書バトは1000km先から帰ってくるといわれている。
   It is said the pigeon _____

2. ハトが帰ってくる可能性は10％である。
   The possibility _____

3. レースについて私に話してくれますか？

4. 私は教室の窓から家へ鳩を飛ばした。(Use "let.")

5. グループワークかペアワークを使ったらどうですか？

Lesson 7

Teaching Reading

リーディングの指導法 ― 文字の識別・読解

　2020年度施行の学習指導要領には,「音声面を中心とした外国語を用いたコミュニケーションを図る素地を育成した上で,高学年において「読むこと」,「書くこと」を加えた教科として外国語科を導入し,5つの領域の言語活動を通して,コミュニケーションを図る基礎となる資質・能力を育成する」という文言があります。従来では「読むこと」,「書くこと」は強調されていませんでしたが,読み書きの能力の必要性が小学校でも求められているのです。

　まず,文字の識別を教えることから始めます。アルファベットの文字AからZまでの文字をアルファベット順に並べたり,文字探しをしたり,文字読み（/ei/ /bi:/ /si:/ /di:/）と音読み（/æ/ /b/ /k/ /d/）があるということを理解させます。それから,大文字と小文字を認識させるゲームなどをして,文字をある程度定着させます。そして,文字の塊である単語を読む練習をします。日本語のひらがなやカタカナは,その一文字一文字が音を表しているので,50音を覚えれば,大体の文字が読めます。しかし,英語は一文字一音の例はあまりなく,単語ごとに発音します。その単語の読み方が語によって違う場合があり,日本人学習者にとって,単語を読むということはかなり負荷がかかります。これまで読まれてきた方法としては,大きく分けてホール・ランゲージ（whole language）とフォニックス（phonics）があります。ホール・ランゲージは文脈から意味を理解・推測させる,そして全体から部分に向かう単語の読み方の一つの指導法です。

　フォニックスとは,一言で言えば,単語の発音とつづり字の結びつきを学習する方法です。アメリカをはじめとするアルファベットを使用する国では,読みを流暢にする一つの方法として,かなり良い結果を生むと考えられています。また,ヘイ（J. Hay）とウィンゴ（C. E. Wingo）によれば,初期の読み方指導に出てくる単語の多くはフォニックスの一般化（generalizations）に当てはまらず,例外も多いので厳選が必要であるといいます。その場合は,サイトワード（sight words）という単語全体で読む方法を取り入れましょう。

　単語が読めたら,今度は文を読むことです。文を読むことには音読と黙読がありますが,児童には,音読が最適です。音読も様々な段階がありますが,まず,文字を見て先生や模範朗読を聞いて繰り返す「リッスン・アンド・リピート」です。形態は「コーラル・リーディング」といってクラスで一斉に元気よく読ませます。「指さし読み」といって文字を指や鉛筆で追いながら読むと,ただの繰り返し（空読み）ではなく,単語を読んでいることになります。全体で読めるようになったら,ペアで助け合う「ペア・リーディング」をさせます。その後,会話などの文は一人一人役を演じる「役割読み」をさせてみましょう。ここまでが文字を音にして児童が一人で読める段階です。

　次は,物語や話の内容を理解する読み方をしてみましょう。内容のある物語などを児童が理解しながら読めるようになるまで,指導者が「読み聞かせ」「ストーリー・テリング」「誘導読み」をしてみましょう。必ず,その際に指導者は児童が内容把握しているか,次は何が起こるかなどを問いかけたり,考えさせたりする活動を行ってください。児童が一人で読む時は自分でも考えながら読むようになるでしょう。そして,児童が一人でまとまった文を内容把握しながら読む段階になったら黙読が良いでしょう。

　このように読みには文字を読む,単語を読む,文を読む,まとまった文章を読むといった段階を踏んだ指導をしましょう。そして読みの究極の目的は,書き手の述べていることを理解し,それについて自分でクリティカル・シンキングをして,自分の考えを持つということです。

Part 2

> アルファベットには2つの読み方があります。児童がそれぞれの読み方ができるように，ABCの歌を2通りの読み方で歌うなど，工夫をしてみましょう。

Let's Talk

ALT: Do you know how to read these letters? (He puts A, B, C, D, E cards on the board.)
HRT: Yes, I do. /ei/, /biː/, /siː/, /diː/, /iː/
ALT: We have different ways of reading. They are /æ/, /b/, /k/, /d/, /e/. /ei/, /biː/, /siː/, /diː/, /iː/ are called alphabet or name sounds. /æ/, /b/, /k/, /d/, /e/ are phonics or /æ/, /b/, /k/, /d/ sounds.
HRT: Oh, I see.
ALT: Let's read this alphabet using phonics. (He puts F to Z on the board.)
HRT: Yes, let's try /æ/, /b/, /k/, /d/, /e/, /f/, /g/, … .

Conversation

Listen to the dialogue and fill in the blanks, then role play the conversation.
会話文を聞いて，空欄に適語を入れなさい。その後，パートナーと会話をしましょう。

HRT: Let's 1._____ letters. This is a 2._____ letter "A." When you read this, it's also 3._____ /æ/. 4._____ after me. /ei/, /ei/, /æ/, /æ/, apple, ant.

Ss: /ei/, /ei/, /æ/, /æ/, apple, ant.

HRT: This is a capital 5._____ "B." /biː/, /biː/, /b/, /b/, bear, banana. Repeat.

Ss: /biː/, /biː/, /b/, /b/, bear, banana.

HRT: What 6._____ start with a "C"?

Ss: Cat, cow, corn.

HRT: Good. What words 7._____ with a "D"?

Ss: Dog, door.

HRT: How do you 8._____ "dog"?

Ss: /diː/-/ou/-/dʒiː/.

HRT: That's right. /d/, /ɑ/, /g/, dog. Good. Please 9._____ the word in your 10._____ .

※ dog の発音は様々ありますが，ここではアメリカ式発音で記載しています。
/dɑg/, /dɔg/, /dá(ː)g/, /dɔ́(ː)g/ 等

Let's Read

Read the passage and answer the questions.
文を読んで次の質問に答えましょう。答えの根拠となる文の行数を（　）に書きましょう。

　When we read Japanese hiragana or katakana, one character is pronounced as a fixed pronunciation. So if you learn fifty (actually forty-five) characters, you can read almost any word written in hiragana or katakana. However, even if you learn to read the 26 English alphabet letters, you cannot read every word in English. When you read English, you have to read the words, which means reading groups of English alphabet letters.　5

　When you read English words, the rules of phonics are useful. If you read A, B, C, D, you will read them as /eɪ/, /biː/, /siː/, /diː/, which are the names of the alphabet. A, B, C, D are also pronounced, /æ/, /b/, /k/, /d/.

　Let's take a look at vowels. The English vowels are a, e, i, o, u and sometimes y. They are pronounced /æ/, /e/, /i/, /ɑ/, /ʌ/. They are called short vowels. They are also　10 pronounced /eɪ/, /iː/, /ɑɪ/, /ou/, /juː/ or /uː/. These are called long vowels. The long vowels are the same as the name of each alphabet letter.

　If the vowel is between consonants, it is pronounced as a short vowel. For example, bat, bet, bit, but, etc. If there is a silent e, the vowel is pronounced as a long vowel. For example, lake, like, etc.　15

　There are many rules about phonics. However, there are also many exceptions that may confuse you. Especially, you can find many exceptions in basic words such as buy, come, could, do, does, done, don't, eight, everyone, father, four, full, give, goes, have, etc. They are words that students should learn as sight words. So when you teach children phonics rules, you have to choose the useful rules carefully. It is said that the　20 more words are used, the more exceptions there are.

(297 words)

1. *Choose the correct statement.*（根拠＿＿行目）
   a. If you learn 26 alphabet letters, you can easily read English words.
   b. Even if you learn 50 Japanese hiragana, you cannot easily read Japanese sentences written in hiragana.
   c. Even if you learn to read 26 English letters, it's difficult to read English words.
2. *What are /eɪ/, /iː/, /ɑɪ/, /ou/, /juː/ or /uː/ called?*（根拠＿＿行目）
   a. They are called long vowels.
   b. They are called double vowels.
   c. They are called short vowels.
3. *Choose the correct statement.*（根拠＿＿行目）
   a. If you learn the rules of phonics, it's easy to read every English word.
   b. Even if you learn every rule of phonics, it's difficult to read every word because there are a lot of exceptions.
   c. There are no exceptions in the rules of phonics.

知っておこう！キーワード　*Choose the correct answer.*　次の語の意味をa〜eの中から選びましょう。

1. alphabet （　　）　2. useful （　　）　3. vowel （　　）　4. consonant （　　）
5. exception （　　）
a. アルファベット　　b. 子音　　c. 例外　　d. 母音　　e. 役に立つ

Part 2

EXERCISES 確認問題
1. *Complete the sentences according to the directions.* 指示に従って文を完成しましょう。
2. *After checking your answers, practice reading the correct sentences aloud.*
答え合わせをしたら，正しい文を音読しましょう。

❶ *Make English sentences using the words below.* T35
日本文を読み，英語の語句を並びかえてください。（文頭は大文字ではありません）

1. "dog" はどうつづりますか？
(how / "dog" / you / spell / do)?
_____

2. 彼は黒板にいくつかカードを貼り付けます。
(some / puts / he / cards / on / board / the).
_____

3. もし，あなたがこれを読むときは，アとも発音されます。
(if / this / you / read /, / also / it's / pronounced / /æ/).
_____

4. "C" で始まる単語は何ですか？
(words / start / with / what / a "C")?
_____

5. あなたはこれらの文字をどう読むかわかりますか？
(There is one word missing.　1語を補ってください。)
(you / read / how / these / know / do / letters)?
_____

❷ *Translate the Japanese sentences into English.* T36
日本文を読み，本文を参考にして英文を書いてください。

1. あなたのノートに単語を写してください。
Please copy _____

2. あなたが英単語を読むときに，フォニックスのルールが役立ちます。
When you _____

3. フォニックスのルールにはあなたを混乱させるかもしれないたくさんの例外もあります。
(Use "may confuse" and "also.")
_____

4. あなたがフォニックスのルールを児童に教えるときは，有用なルールを厳選する必要があります。
_____

5. 言葉は多く使われるほど，より多くの例外があるといわれています。
_____

Teaching Reading **39**

Lesson 8

Teaching Writing

> ライティングの指導法 — 大文字・小文字，語句や表現

　英語学習の4技能の中では，ライティングを教えるのが一番難しいといわれています。日本の中学，高校の英語の授業や日常生活でも英語を書く機会は限られています。

　2020年度施行の学習指導要領の小学校外国語科においては，「書くこと」を指導することが求められており，以下のア），イ）の項目が挙げられています。

ア）　大文字，小文字を活字体で書くことができるようにする。また，語順を意識しながら音声で十分に慣れ親しんだ簡単な語句や基本的な表現を書き写すことができるようにする。

イ）　自分のことや身近で簡単な事柄について，例文を参考に，音声で十分に慣れ親しんだ簡単な語句や基本的な表現を用いて書くことができるようにする。

　「書く」領域の活動は，言語の書記記号（文字）にかかわる側面と書記記号を道具として意思を表現・伝達する側面を持っているといわれています。すなわち「筆写」と「作文」です。上のア）は「書写」で，イ）は「作文」にあたります。基礎としての書写が十分にできることが重要となります。

　書写の段階では，児童が楽しみながら書き写すことが大事です。まず，ABCの26文字を発音させて書く練習をします。声を出させて書く練習をさせるとよいでしょう。4線のペンマンシップのノートに書くと，それぞれの文字の位置が確認できると思います。小文字はローマ字を第3学年で学習しているのである程度書くことができるでしょう。まず，単語，次に語句，文，最後に文章を写すなど，段階を追った指導が求められます。

　また，書くことを指導する前に，文字について興味を持たせることがとても大事です。アルファベットのAは，牛の頭を逆さにしたものからきた象形文字であるということを話したり，大文字と小文字はなぜあるのだろうと問いかけたりすることが考えられます。大文字は文頭，固有名詞の語頭，頭文字（UNESCO，IOC），題名の内容語の語頭，曜日，月名，一人称単数のIなどに使われます。そのことなどから興味を持たせ，「書写」を「作文」につなげるといった知的好奇心を引き起こし，書くことに抵抗を持たせないようにすることが肝要です。

　作文は，簡単な文の発音がしっかりとでき，その文を十分に書き写すことができてから，My name is Chris. など模範文を与えます。その名前を自分の名前に書き換えさせたり，自分の住んでいる場所について模範文を書き換えさせたり，自己紹介文から作文を始めると良いでしょう。名前や日本の地名は既習のローマ字で書くことができます。その際に，ローマ字が英文に現れるときは，訓令式でなく，一般的にヘボン式ローマ字であることを確認させる必要があります。その後，誕生カードやオリジナル絵本の作成をさせたり，低学年の児童に読み聞かせを行うといった活動に発展させることができます。

　小学校におけるライティングの指導では，まず，書写がしっかりできるように指導することが大切です。その後，例文を参考に自分自身の文が書けるようになれば理想的です。

Part 2

> 文字を導入するときには，児童が書くことに負担を感じないようにする必要があります。

Let's Talk

HRT: Teaching writing to students is very difficult, but important.
ALT: Yes, at first we teach them the alphabet.
HRT: However, we should avoid making them dislike English by teaching them how to write.
ALT: Of course, we have to have them be interested in writing.
HRT: Let's ask them to collect English words written on signboards. They will be interested in the English alphabet.
ALT: That's a good idea.

Conversation

Listen to the dialogue and fill in the blanks, then role play the conversation.
会話文を聞いて，空欄に適語を入れなさい。その後，パートナーと会話をしましょう。

ALT: You studied Roman letters two years ago. Do you remember how many letters there are in the English alphabet?

S1: I 1._____ about the alphabet. But I know we have 50 hiragana in Japanese.

ALT: There are 2._____ letters in English. The total is 26 letters. 〈Showing the alphabet〉

S1: I 3._____ that. I can read most of them.

ALT: Do you know 4._____ the letter A came from?

Ss: I don't know.

ALT: It came from the head of a cow. 〈Shows the picture. Then turns it upside down.〉 Is it 5._____ to the letter A? The letter B is from a house.

S2: Wow! 6._____ ! It's like "kawa (川)" in Japanese. Or "yama (山)." Or "ki (木)."

ALT: Good! It is called a 7._____ . Let's write the letter A in the air saying A. 〈They write A in the air〉 Then B, and so on. OK. Can you write them in your 8._____ ?

Ss: Yes, we can.

ALT: So these are all called 9._____ letters. When do you see capital letters?

Ss: Name. 文のはじまり。JR, NHK, IOC, JAL, ANA.

ALT: Great! Do you know 10._____ type of letter?

S3: Yes, *komoji*, small letters.

Let's Read

Read the passage and answer the questions.
文を読んで次の質問に答えましょう。答えの根拠となる文の行数を（　）に書きましょう。

When children begin to study writing in English in elementary school, they will be introduced to the alphabet letters first, and then simple words and easy sentences. Actually, most students had already written Roman letters when they were in the third grade. But most of them don't remember writing all the alphabet letters with the exception of writing their own names. They don't even realize that Roman letters and the alphabet are the same 5 thing. Therefore, at the beginning of writing time, a teacher should carefully show how to write each letter. Sometimes before asking them to write the letters, the teacher should show the letter with gestures, which is so much fun for the kids. The teacher can also check whether the kids write the letter with the correct stroke order.

After children can write the alphabet, they start to write simple words and phrases. 10 According to government guidelines, before they start writing, they should listen to English words and expressions many times. Then, when they become accustomed to the words, they can start writing them. However, there is not really enough time for children to learn by input alone. Also, kids like to try to write in English as soon as they hear a word. Some of them are excited to try to write what they hear in class. They want to take 15 notes of unknown words. Teachers should therefore allow them to write when they feel interested in writing, even if they misspell the word. Such students will be interested in writing by being encouraged by teachers.

(260 words)

1. *When did the students start writing Roman letters?* （根拠　　行目）
   a. When they were in the first grade
   b. When they were in the third grade
   c. They haven't learned Roman letters yet.
2. *Choose the correct statement.* （根拠　　行目）
   a. According to government guidelines, children should listen first, and write later.
   b. Children must learn how to write before they listen to words and phrases.
   c. Teachers should begin teaching writing when the students are in the third grade.
3. *Choose the correct statement.* （根拠　　行目）
   a. Every kid doesn't like writing.
   b. Teachers should stop children writing when they make a mistake.
   c. Kids like to try to write in English as soon as they hear a word.

| 知っておこう！キーワード | *Choose the correct answer.* 次の語の意味をa〜eの中から選びましょう。 |

1. signboard (　)　　2. capital letter (　)　　3. small letter (　)
4. pictograph (　)　　5. Roman letter (　)
a. 小文字　　b. 看板　　c. ローマ字　　d. 大文字　　e. 象形文字

Part 2

> **EXERCISES** 確認問題
> 1. *Complete the sentences according to the directions.* 指示に従って文を完成しましょう。
> 2. *After checking your answers, practice reading the correct sentences aloud.*
> 答え合わせをしたら，正しい文を音読しましょう。

❶ *Make English sentences using the words below.* T40
日本文を読み，英語の語句を並びかえてください。（文頭は大文字ではありません）

1. 英語には文字がより少ない。
(there / English / are / letters / in / fewer).
_____

2. 私たちは，まず，児童にアルファベットを教えます。
(first / at / the / students / teach / alphabet / we).
_____

3. ほとんどの児童がすべてのアルファベットを書いたことを覚えていない。
(alphabet / students / don't / writing / all / the / remember / letters / most of the).
_____

4. 児童に書き方を教えることにより，英語を嫌いにさせるのを避けなければならない。
(write / English / should / students / them / we / by / how / dislike / to / avoid / making / teaching).
_____

5. 児童はローマ字とアルファベットが同じだということに気づいてさえいない。
(realize / letters / even / alphabet / the / are / the / and / Roman / don't / students / that). (There is one word missing. 1語を補ってください。)
_____

❷ *Translate the Japanese sentences into English.* T41
日本文を読み，本文を参考にして英文を書いてください。

1. それらは大文字と呼ばれます。
They _____

2. 児童は英語のアルファベットに興味を持つでしょう。
_____

3. 教師はそれぞれの文字の書き方を注意深く教える必要があります。
A teacher should _____

4. 児童は書き始める前に，英語の単語や表現を何回も聞くべきです。
Before the students start writing, _____

5. （ある児童は）授業で聞いたことを書こうとすることにワクワクします。
Some of the students _____

Teaching Writing 43

Part 3　活動・教材・教具

Lesson 9

Activities to Get Children Involved (1)

> リズム・メロディを通した活動 ― 歌・チャンツを用いて

　リズム・メロディを通した活動は，歌やチャンツを用いて行うとよいでしょう。英語には特有の音変化があり，英語らしい発音をしようとすると「母語の干渉」といい，母語である日本語がそれを妨げることがあります。しかし，歌はメロディやリズムに乗りながら言葉を発するので，自然で英語らしい発音に近づけることができます。

　英語では童謡を Nursery Rhymes と呼び，親しまれている伝承童謡は Mother Goose と呼ばれます。Mother Goose には，日本の童謡と同じように，子守歌，遊び歌，数え歌，なぞなぞ歌，早口歌，積み上げ歌など，様々なものがあります。小学校英語では童謡以外にポップス音楽を教材として取り上げることもできます。ポップスの中には，スピードが適切でメロディが親しみやすく，子どもが共感できる歌詞のものも多くあります。過去のスタンダード・ナンバーから現代の流行りの曲まで，教材として相応しいと思う曲を日頃から探しておくと良いでしょう。英語の歌を歌う利点は，授業で一斉にクラス単位で英語の歌を歌うので，人前で英語を話すことと比べ，周りの反応が気にならないことです。気持ちがリラックスした状態になり，楽しみながら積極的に英語に触れることができるでしょう。また，メロディとともに英語の歌詞を記憶するので，歌詞の中にある文法や文型事項を定着する手助けもしてくれます。低年齢の子どもにおいては，「全身反応法」といって手遊びや動作と共に英語の歌を歌う方法を用い，自然に言葉を理解しながら歌うよう指導するのも良いでしょう。しかし，認知がより発達した高学年の児童にはあまり適さない場合があるので，配慮や工夫が必要です。また，外国語の歌を歌うことの利点は言語学習だけに限りません。友情や平和，異文化理解など，様々なテーマの歌を歌うことで，自己肯定感や多様な価値観を認める姿勢を身につける機会となるでしょう。

　次にチャンツです。チャンツとは，元来，聖歌などの歌やお経を意味する chant の複数形です。英語教育ではチャンツというと，メロディを付けずに，英語のフレーズや文章をリズミカルに読んだり歌ったりする活動のことを指します。チャンツも歌と同じように，母語の干渉を受けずに自然に発音できるようになる方法です。歌と違いメロディがなく，韻を踏む必要もないので単語を並べるだけで行えます。簡単に英語学習に取り入れることが可能です。チャンツを行うには，手拍子や机を叩くなどをしてビートを刻みます。児童の反応を見ながら速さを調節します。長い文の場合は短い文節から始め，次第に文節を長くします。それを繰り返すことで，結果として，まとまりのある文章を英語らしく発音することにつながるのです。

Part 3

英語や外国語の歌は，実際に授業で歌うだけでなく，歌詞の内容にも注目しましょう。言語間における表現の違いや相似性を発見することにより，異文化理解の学びにつながるからです。

Let's Talk

HRT: Do you know the song "Old MacDonald Had a Farm"?
  S: Yes. I know the Japanese version.
HRT: Oh, do you? So what is the song about?
  S: Animals?
HRT: Right. The song has many sounds of animals, such as pigs and horses.

Conversation

Listen to the dialogue and fill in the blanks, then role play the conversation.
会話文を聞いて，空欄に適語を入れなさい。その後，パートナーと会話をしましょう。

HRT: Now, 1._____ watch a video of "Old MacDonald Had a Farm."
Ss: Yes!

───〈After watching video〉───

HRT: What kinds 2._____ animals did you see? Are there any animals 3._____ for pigs, horses, and ducks?
S1: Dogs, cats, cows, chickens, and sheep.
HRT: Good. What 4._____ did the cats make?
S2: Meow-meow.
HRT: Yes. It sounds 5._____ to the Japanese word. What about dogs?
S3: Bow-wow.
HRT: Yes. Does it sound similar to the Japanese one?
Ss: No.
HRT: What sound do dogs make 6._____ Japanese?
Ss: Wan-wan!
HRT: Right. Do you know what sound dogs 7._____ in Chinese?
S4: Wan-wan?
HRT: Yes, it sounds 8._____ the same as the one they make in Japanese. They go wàng- wàng in Chinese.
S5: That's very interesting.
HRT: Right. It's fascinating to know animal sounds in 9._____ languages.
S6: Yes. Can we learn 10._____ tomorrow, too?
HRT: Why not?

Activities to Get Children Involved (1) **47**

Let's Read

Read the passage and answer the questions.
文を読んで次の質問に答えましょう。答えの根拠となる文の行数を（　）に書きましょう。

Nursery rhymes are poems or songs sung to small children. Most people have heard lullabies when they were small children. Lullabies are songs to help a child fall asleep, and they are often nursery rhymes. Many nursery rhymes are loved by small children, their parents, or nursery school teachers. Why do they sing nursery rhymes? And why are nursery rhymes so effective for learning language? 5

You can hear repetition of similar sounds or the same sounds in English songs. This is called rhyming. For example, "Twinkle, twinkle, little star. How I wonder what you are." You can see that "star" and "are" rhyme in this verse. As small children hear the sounds many times, they can learn the sound along with the music. The next line is "Up above the world so high, like a diamond in the sky." Along with the rhyming, there is 10 also a phrase often used in speech; "in the sky." Nursery rhymes help children expand their vocabulary and expressions in their speech.

These are only a couple of reasons why nursery rhymes are good for small children. But there is another, simpler reason why they are effective: Nursery rhymes are fun. Children have fun singing. They can imagine the story in the songs in their head. You 15 may also notice that they sometimes change words or entire sections of the songs. Nursery rhymes provide a place where children can play with words. When this happens, children will want to learn new words and phrases.

(249 words)

1. *What are lullabies?* （根拠　　行目）
   a. Songs to help parents fall asleep
   b. Songs to help children fall asleep
   c. Songs to help children wake up
2. *Which of the following words rhyme?* （根拠　　行目）
   a. Star and are　　b. Twinkle and star　　c. Up and so
3. *What do nursery rhymes provide for children?* （根拠　　行目）
   a. A place where children can go overseas
   b. A place where children can run in the playground
   c. A place where children can play with words

知っておこう！キーワード　*Choose the correct answer.*　次の語の意味をa～eの中から選びましょう。

1. rhyme (　)　　2. verse (　)　　3. repetition (　)　　4. poem (　)
5. phrase (　)
a. 成句　　b. 繰り返し　　c. 詩　　d. 韻を踏む　　e. 歌の一節

Part 3

EXERCISES 確認問題
1. *Complete the sentences according to the directions.* 指示に従って文を完成しましょう。
2. *After checking your answers, practice reading the correct sentences aloud.*
   答え合わせをしたら，正しい文を音読しましょう。

❶ *Make English sentences using the words below.*
日本文を読み，英語の語句を並びかえてください。（文頭は大文字ではありません）

1. どんな動物を見ましたか？
   (animals / see / what / did / of / you / kinds)?
   _____

2. 猫は英語でミャオミャオと鳴きます。
   (go / English / meow-meow / cats / in).
   _____

3. 豚，馬，アヒル以外で他の動物はいますか？
   (pigs, / any / except / ducks / are / for / animals / horses, / there / and)?
   _____

4. 外国語で動物の鳴き声を知るのはおもしろいですね。
   (is / animal / fascinating / languages / it / to / know / in / foreign / sounds).
   _____

5. あなたは英語の歌の中で似ている音や同じ音の繰り返しを聴くことができます。
   (There is one word missing.　1語を補ってください。)
   (can / repetition / hear / or / sounds / similar / the / songs / sounds / English / in / you / same).
   _____

❷ *Translate the Japanese sentences into English.*
日本文を読み，本文を参考にして英文を書いてください。

1. 子ども達は歌うことを楽しみます。
   Children _____

2. 明日もさらに学ぶことができますか？
   Can we _____

3. ほとんどの人々は幼い頃，子守歌を聴いたことがあります。(Use "heard" and "small.")
   _____

4. Old MacDonald Had a Farm の映像を見ましょう。(Use "watch" and "of.")
   _____

5. 中国語で犬はどう鳴くか知っていますか？(Use "know" and "make.")
   _____

Lesson 10

Activities to Get Children Involved (2)

知的好奇心を刺激する活動 ― ゲーム・クイズ を用いて

　小学校で初めて英語を学ぶ児童にとって，授業に対し不安や緊張を感じてしまうことは珍しくありません。児童の興味を喚起し，楽しい授業作りのために，ゲームやクイズは欠かせない活動の一つでもあります。学習者が人前で間違えることを恐れ，負の感情から学習を阻害するといわれている情意フィルターを働かせないためにも，効果的な学習活動にもつながります。しかしながら，ここで注意したいのは，学習者の年齢や発達段階における認知発達レベルです。小学校で英語を教える時期は中学年から高学年にわたる幅広い年齢，かつ，著しい認知発達が進む時でもあります。中学年では，賑やかな学習活動でも児童が問題なく楽しんで参加することが多いですが，個人差はあるにせよ，高学年ではそういった活動を楽しまない傾向があります。その理由として，母語で高度な思考を働かせることが可能になり，分析や論理的思考，現実に根差した学習を好むようになるからと説明されています。したがって，どの学年に対しても，楽しさ重視のゲームやクイズを行うのではなく，それぞれの発達段階に応じた学習活動や知的好奇心を刺激する活動を考える必要があります。では，実際中学年，高学年に分け，どのようなゲームやクイズがあるのか紹介します。

　中学年では，Simon Says Game という学習活動があります。教師が"Simon Says"を言った場合のみ，命令にしたがって動く「全身反応法」のゲームです。ただ，児童はすぐにこのゲームに慣れ，中には飽きてしまう児童も出始めるので，教師がスピードを上げて命令する，引っ掛け問題を出すなどの工夫が必要になります。他には，中学年で動物名を学習した後，ジェスチャーで何の動物かを当てるジェスチャー・ゲームという学習活動があります。児童をいくつかのグループに分け，一人ずつ，一つの動物の特徴をジェスチャーで表し，他の子どもが動物名を当てていきます。動物によっては単純なジェスチャーでは，表し難いものもあるので趣向を凝らさなければならないでしょう。

　高学年では，数字あてクイズという数字を使った学習で，物の数，高さ，重さを推測させるクイズも良いでしょう。例えば，人が1年間のうちに消費するビニール袋や割り箸の数を考えさせ，実際の数を知ることで，環境に対する意識を持つことにつながります。このように高学年の児童にゲームやクイズをする際は，彼らの認知発達に合った内容にすると良いでしょう。教科横断型内容（L.13後述）やテーマに沿った学習内容を取り入れることで，彼らの思考力を育む活動が期待できます。

　ゲームやクイズを授業で行う際には，「言語教育」を行うという視点を持ち，ただ楽しいだけでない，子どもの知的好奇心を喚起できる活動を取り入れると良いでしょう。

Part 3

> ゲームやクイズをする際，事前の活動として，実際に教師がお手本を示すことを忘れてはいけません。口頭説明だけでなく，児童に活動方法を見せ，言葉を聞かせることで，理解を促すことが期待できます。

Let's Talk

HRT: Let's count from one to twenty.
　Ss: One, two, three, four ... twenty.
HRT: Look at these chopsticks. How many chopsticks do you see?
　S: Thirteen?
HRT: No. The answer is fifteen.

Conversation

Listen to the dialogue and fill in the blanks, then role play the conversation.
会話文を聞いて，空欄に適語を入れなさい。その後，パートナーと会話をしましょう。

HRT: Look at these things. What are they?
　S1: Chopsticks?
HRT: Right. Where do you get chopsticks?
　S2: At a 1._____ store?
HRT: Yes. Do you 2._____ them?
　S2: No.
HRT: Unfortunately, we 3._____ them away after we use them. They are called 4._____ chopsticks.
　S3: Disposable?
HRT: It 5._____ we throw them away. How 6._____ disposable chopsticks do you use a year? Make a 7._____ .
　S4: Twenty?
HRT: It 8._____ said that an average person uses about two hundred disposable chopsticks a year.
　S5: Two hundred! What a waste!
HRT: What can you do to 9._____ waste?
　S6: We can carry our 10._____ chopsticks with us.
HRT: That's a great idea.

Let's Read

Read the passage and answer the questions.
文を読んで次の質問に答えましょう。答えの根拠となる文の行数を（ ）に書きましょう。

  Chris White teaches English with the fifth-grade teacher, Ms. Sato. One day they talked about a lesson plan for the fifth-grade class. They wanted to try an activity that hadn't been done yet in class. Their students had already learned words for colors, food, numbers, shapes, and seasons. Mr. White and Ms. Sato wanted to make an activity that helped the students to bring out the vocabulary they already knew.   5

  Mr. White came up with an activity that they had never tried in class and that would allow the students to use the words they had learned. He explained to Ms. Sato about the game. "It's a kind of guessing game similar to Three Hint Quiz, but you have to prepare photos or pictures to show beforehand. I would recommend bringing photos of vegetables to show the students. The students are familiar with a lot of English words for 10 food already. First, the students make pairs. One of the students in the pair closes their eyes. You then show the other students a photo. After five seconds, you hide the photo, and the students with their eyes closed are allowed to open them and ask questions to their partner about the thing in the photo. Here is an important tip. Tell all of the students the category of the thing before starting the game. For example, tell them the thing is a 15 vegetable. Otherwise, they have no idea what to ask their partner."

  Ms. Sato liked the idea of the guessing game because her students were used to answering questions, and they were also old enough to ask questions by themselves. Besides, it enabled the students to produce words or sentences without preparation. She looked forward to trying the game for her class the following week. (296 words) 20

1. *What did Ms. Sato and Mr. White want the students to do?*（根拠＿＿行目）
    a. They wanted the students to like vegetables.
    b. They wanted the students to use the vocabulary they knew.
    c. They wanted the students to try some new food.
2. *Why did Mr. White recommend using the words of vegetables for the game?*
    （根拠＿＿行目）
    a. Because those words were familiar to the students
    b. Because those words were popular with their students
    c. Because those words were important to review
3. *Ms. Sato liked the guessing game because …*（根拠＿＿行目）
    a. the students were used to asking questions by themselves.
    b. the students could produce words or sentences without preparation.
    c. the students had already tried the food.

知っておこう！キーワード | *Choose the correct answer.* 次の語の意味をa〜eの中から選びましょう。

1. category （ ）   2. produce （ ）   3. tip （ ）   4. preparation （ ）
5. bring out （ ）
a. 準備   b. コツ   c.（言葉を）引き出す   d. 産みだす   e. 種類

Part 3

EXERCISES 確認問題
1. *Complete the sentences according to the directions.* 指示に従って文を完成しましょう。
2. *After checking your answers, practice reading the correct sentences aloud.*
   答え合わせをしたら，正しい文を音読しましょう。

❶ *Make English sentences using the words below.* T50
   日本文を読み，英語の語句を並びかえてください。(文頭は大文字ではありません)

   1. もったいないです。
      (a / what / waste) !
      _____

   2. その箸を再利用しますか？
      (reuse / you / chopsticks / the / do)?
      _____

   3. 彼は一つの活動を思いつきました。
      (activity / an / came / he / up / with).
      _____

   4. あなたは写真や絵を準備しなくてはいけません。
      (have / or / photos / prepare / pictures / to / you).
      _____

   5. 児童たちは相手に何を聞けばよいかまったくわかりません。
      (There is one word missing. 1語を補ってください。)
      (ask / to / partner / have / their / no / students / the / idea).
      _____

❷ *Translate the Japanese sentences into English.* T51
   日本文を読み，本文を参考にして英文を書いてください。

   1. ここに大切なコツがあります。
      Here's _____

   2. 彼女はそのゲームを試すことを楽しみにして待ちました。
      She looked _____

   3. 無駄を減らすためにあなたは何ができますか？(Use "reduce" and "what.")
      _____

   4. 1年でストローを何本使いますか？(Use "straws" and "many.")
      _____

   5. 平均的な人は1年で約200膳の使い捨て箸を使うといわれています。(Use "said" and "average.")
      _____

Lesson 11

Activities to Get Children Involved (3)

デジタル教材を活かした活動 ― ICT・映像を用いて

　デジタル教材とは，教科書や副教材をデジタル化し，電子黒板やパソコンを使用してスクリーンに画像や映像を表示できる教材を意味します。ICT は「information and communication technology」の略で，日本語では「情報通信技術」と訳されます。ICT を使った教材（以下 ICT 教材）は電子黒板だけでなく，プロジェクター，教科書準拠デジタルコンテンツ，インターネットなど，多くの電子機器や通信技術が含まれます。学校の教室にもデジタル教材や ICT 化の波が押し寄せ，教師はより一層工夫を凝らした教材研究の必要性が求められています。

　文部科学省が作成した教材を採用した場合，それに準拠するデジタル教材が配布されます。使用するには，初めにデジタル教材のソフトをパソコンにインストールし，パソコンを電子黒板やプロジェクターに接続します。こういった過程を経て，ようやくスクリーン上で絵，写真，文字の提示，映像や音声の視聴ができるようになります。中にはパソコンが不要な電子黒板もありますので確認しましょう。

　さて，インターネット環境が整っている教室であれば，世界中で共有されている画像や動画も教材として利用することができます。教材用動画サイトは，その用法を守れば授業で使うのに問題はありませんが，YouTube などの動画共有サイトは著作権を侵害している違法動画も多くあります。授業で動画共有サイトを使用するには注意が必要です。

　インターネット電話は，海外にいる姉妹校の子どもたちと声や映像を使って，触れ合える便利なツールでもあります。児童が何を話して良いかわからない場合が多くありますので，事前にテーマを決めて考えさせ，準備や練習をする時間を設け，通話時に発表形式の Show and Tell をするのも良いでしょう。異文化理解につながる活動が期待できます。

　パソコンのスライド使用により，教師の板書にかかる時間と労力はかなり短縮できました。しかし，スライドを見ている側は，受身の態勢になり，次第に退屈することも少なくないので使用方法に工夫が必要です。適度なスライド提示時間を保ち，児童が自ら積極的に動く学習活動へと導いていくことが求められます。

　学習障害を持つ児童は文字の読み書きに困難さを感じます。しかし，デジタル教材やスライドを使用することで，文字を大きくすることや，行間を広くすること，分かち書きに書くことなど，工夫を凝らした表示が可能になり，学習内容がわかりやすくなる場合もあります。それぞれの児童が持つ困難さに対応するために，適切かつ適度なデジタル教材や ICT 教材の使用を心がけて，授業作りをすると良いでしょう。

Part 3

電子黒板のスクリーンやパソコンのスライドでアルファベットを表示する場合，児童にとって見やすいフォントや色を選び，文字サイズを大きくすることを忘れないようにしましょう。

Let's Talk

T52
S32

HRT: Now I will show you seven letters of the alphabet on the screen. You have only ten seconds to remember them.
S: Only ten seconds?
HRT: Yes. You can write the letters on your worksheets after they disappear from the screen. Then talk to your partner. You can ask them questions and tell them what letters you remembered.

Conversation

T53
S33

Listen to the dialogue and fill in the blanks, then role play the conversation.
会話文を聞いて，空欄に適語を入れなさい。その後，パートナーと会話をしましょう。

HRT: You only have ten 1._____ to remember the seven letters on the screen. Are you ready?
Ss: Yes!

──〈Ten seconds later〉──

HRT: First, try 2._____ remember the letters you saw. Then write them in your 3._____ . Are you finished 4._____ the letters?
Ss: Yes.
HRT: Are you ready to exchange information 5._____ your partner?
S1: Not really. I already forgot some of them.
HRT: You don't 6._____ to worry. I'm sure your 7._____ will help you. OK?
S1: OK.
S2: I saw "e," "g," "h," "i," "l," and "n." Only one letter is 8._____ .
S1: Oh, I saw "s," too.
S1&2: We found seven 9._____ !
HRT: Let's check the answers. The answers are "e," "g," "h," "i," "l," "n," and "s."
S1&2: We got it right!
HRT: Do you know what word you can 10._____ with these seven letters?
S2: English!
HRT: Great work!

Activities to Get Children Involved (3)

Let's Read

Read the passage and answer the questions.
文を読んで次の質問に答えましょう。答えの根拠となる文の行数を（　）に書きましょう。

T54
S34

　　Ms. Sato used to handcraft alphabet cards and picture cards for her English lesson. But she felt that it wasted a lot of time and paper. Ms. Sato knew that Mr. White made slides for alphabet cards and picture cards on a computer. Ms. Sato decided to talk to him to improve her lesson.

　　"Hi, Mr. White. Can you show me your slides for your English lesson?" asked Ms. Sato. "Oh, good timing Ms. Sato. I am about to make slides for tomorrow's lesson. You can watch," he answered. "Thank you," said Ms. Sato. "No problem. Today the students learned numbers, so I am going to do a quiz to review numbers with them tomorrow. I will show the students videos of scenes with people buying food in English. First I will show it to them without the sound, and then I will have them guess how much of something the person bought. Let's have a look at a video of someone buying some ham without the sound. How much ham do you think the person bought?" he said. Ms. Sato watched the video and could see the size of the pack of ham the person bought. She guessed, "300 grams?" "No, actually it's 600 grams. I'll show you the video with sound. Now you can hear the person ordering 600 grams," Mr. White said. "Wow, this is fun," she said. He continued, "Yes. The students can enjoy guessing different numbers. It's easy to make slides that play videos with or without sound. Also, seeing what people buy and how much they buy will help the students understand how people live in different countries."

　　On the way home, Ms. Sato was feeling good because she learned how to make good use of slides. She thought she could depend on other teachers if she needed help.　(305 words)

5

10

15

20

1. *Why did Ms. Sato decide to ask Mr. White about his slides?* （根拠＿＿行目）
   a. Because she wanted to make her lessons better
   b. Because she wanted to be positive
   c. Because she wanted to watch videos on the computer
2. *What could the students learn by seeing people in other countries buy food?*
   （根拠＿＿行目）
   a. They could learn how to play videos without sounds.
   b. They could learn about how people live in different countries.
   c. They could learn how to cook different types of food.
3. *How did Ms. Sato feel after she asked Mr. White about his lessons?* （根拠＿＿行目）
   a. She was disappointed with his opinion and what he showed her on the computer.
   b. She found it a waste of time because he gave her too much information.
   c. She felt it was helpful asking him about how to make good use of slides.

知っておこう！キーワード	*Choose the correct answer.*　次の語の意味をa〜eの中から選びましょう。

1. slide (　　)　2. without sound (　　)　3. screen (　　)　4. handcraft (　　)
5. video (　　)
a. 動画　　b. 手作りする　　c. スライド　　d. スクリーン　　e. 無音で

Part 3

> **EXERCISES** 確認問題
> 1. *Complete the sentences according to the directions.* 指示に従って文を完成しましょう。
> 2. *After checking your answers, practice reading the correct sentences aloud.*
>   答え合わせをしたら，正しい文を音読しましょう。

❶ *Make English sentences using the words below.* T55
日本文を読み，英語の語句を並びかえてください。（文頭は大文字ではありません）

1. それからノートにその文字を書き出します。
   (write / notebook / your / in / letters / then / the).
   _____

2. 文字は書き終わりましたか？
   (finished / writing / letters / are / you / the)?
   _____

3. まず，見た文字を思い出してみましょう。
   (saw / remember / to / first / you / letters / try / the / ,).
   _____

4. パートナーと情報交換をする用意はできていますか？
   (with / information / ready / exchange / are / your / to / you / partner)?
   _____

5. スクリーン上に映る７つの文字を覚えるのは 10 秒の間だけです。
   (There is one word missing. 1 語を補ってください。)
   (on / seconds / ten / the / to / screen / you / only / letters / have / seven / the).
   _____

❷ *Translate the Japanese sentences into English.* T56
日本文を読み，本文を参考にして英文を書いてください。

1. 心配はいりません。
   You don't _____

2. きっとあなたのパートナーが手助けしてくれますよ。
   I'm sure _____

3. 一文字だけ足りません。
   Only _____

4. 私はもうすでにその中のいくつかの文字を忘れました。(Use "some" and "letters.")
   _____

5. これらの７文字で何の言葉をつづれるかわかりますか？(Use "spell" and "with.")
   _____

Activities to Get Children Involved (3)

Lesson 12

Developing Children's Thinking Skills (1)

> 考えさせる指導法（1）— 自発的に学び，考える力を育む

　母語の自然な習得過程においても，乳幼児は，言葉を聞くだけではなく，見る触れるなど身体の感覚のすべてを使って情報を得，インタラクションをしながら脳内で情報を整理し処理することでコミュニケーション能力を身につけていきます。さらに，それらの情報は言語習得だけに限らず，認知発達，身体発達，社会適応など，様々な形で人間の育成に関わっていきます。外国語の学習も，他教科と同様，小学生が心身ともに健やかに育つための授業として位置づけられ，言語，文化，社会，人間，自分のアイデンティティなどを考える良い機会となることでしょう。

　文部科学省は，2020年度施行の学習指導要領において，「全ての教科などにおいて ①知識及び技能，②思考力，判断力，表現力等，③学びに向かう力，人間性等の三つの柱で整理する」と述べ（2017年），「すべての子どもに，課題解決のために自ら考え判断・行動できる『社会を生き抜く力』を育成しよう」としています。さらに，「これからの社会を生きる子供たちは，自ら課題を発見し解決する力，コミュニケーション能力，物事を多様な観点から考察する力（クリティカル・シンキング），様々な情報を取捨選択できる力などが求められると考えられます」とも述べており，外国語教育でも広く深い思考につながる指導が必要とされています。

　2018年度に移行措置として文部科学省が作成した教材『Let's Try!』，『We Can!』では，新たな活動 "Let's Watch and Think" が導入されました。例えば，デジタル教材の映像を視聴して内容を聞き取るだけでなく，発展的な活動を通して，自発的な気づきを促し，自分の意見を持ち，それを述べることが想定されています。

　それでは，指導者は具体的にどのような活動ができるでしょうか。音声や動画などのデジタル教材を利用し，体験型の授業作りができますが，単なる内容理解だけではなく，理解した後の活動が重要となってきます。例えば，初めて英語に触れるであろう3年生の教材『Let's Try!』の最初のユニットでのデジタル教材では，世界の様々な挨拶を映像とともに紹介し，児童に言語や文化の違いや共通点に気づかせ，地球の一員であることについて考えさせています。一方で，高学年では，教材『We Can!』において，丁寧な表現から社会的な対応を学んだり，また海外について視聴理解するだけでなく，自分の将来の夢につなげるなど，さらに児童に考えさせるような指導が必要になります。

Part 3

視聴覚教材を使う場合の導入や，児童から発話を引き出す会話を学びましょう。児童に作表をいきなりさせるのではなく，黒板やスクリーン上で，聞こえた単語を確認し，並べて見せます。表を見ながら違いに気づかせ，最後に意見を述べさせます。

Let's Talk

HRT: Let's watch a video today.
 Ss: Yes! Great!
 S1: What kind of video is it?
HRT: It's about summer vacations in the world.
 S2: Summer … ?
HRT: Well, let's play the video. Watch and tell me what you see. Are you ready?
 Ss: Yes!

Conversation

Listen to the dialogue and fill in the blanks, then role play the conversation.
会話文を聞いて，空欄に適語を入れなさい。その後，パートナーと会話をしましょう。

〈After watching a video about summer vacations, the teacher puts an empty comparison table on the blackboard.〉

T: Let's fill in this comparison 1.＿＿＿＿＿＿＿＿ now.
Ss: Yes, of course!
T: Do you know what a table is?
Ss: *Tsukue*!
T: That's right, but there is 2.＿＿＿＿＿＿＿＿ meaning. Look at the blackboard. This is also 3.＿＿＿＿＿＿＿＿ a "table." OK, which countries are these?
Ss: America! Australia! Singapore!
T: Yes, great! You 4.＿＿＿＿＿＿＿＿ them. 5.＿＿＿＿＿＿＿＿ put the countries' names here. Did you 6.＿＿＿＿＿＿＿＿ anything else from the video? Tell me what you heard.
Ss: Vacation! Homework! July, September … Camp!

―――〈After completing the comparison table〉―――

T: 7.＿＿＿＿＿＿＿＿ made a great one. Let's 8.＿＿＿＿＿＿＿＿ what is different. Look … here … and here.
Ss: December … Australia … six weeks … no homework.
T: That's right. They have summer vacation in December in Australia 9.＿＿＿＿＿＿＿＿ six weeks. They have 10.＿＿＿＿＿＿＿＿ homework.

Developing Children's Thinking Skills (1) 59

Let's Read

Read the passage and answer the questions.
文を読んで次の質問に答えましょう。答えの根拠となる文の行数を（　）に書きましょう。

　　In this modern world with the Internet, children are under the threat of information overload from SNS and video applications every day. No one can deny that it is crucial to develop "critical thinking skills" in education, and the earlier, the better. Children must learn how to recognize what is true and useful information by themselves.

　　In English lessons, there are six questions we can use; who, what, where, when, why, and how. These questions are not difficult and give learners a chance to think and reflect.
- Who said it? (A famous person? A friend?—Does it matter who said it?)
- What did they say? (Is there any proof? Based on a fact?—Is it true?)
- Where did they say it? (Public or private?—Any counter-opinion from the other side?)
- When did they say it? (Before, after, or during school or an event?)
- Why did they say it? (Were they trying to make someone good or bad?)
- How did they say it? (Did they speak it or write it? Were they happy, sad, or angry?)

　　They might not be able to answer by themselves first and might ask you many questions. You might not want to be bothered by those questions, but don't worry, it does not continue for long. They will get used to asking questions themselves and make it their habit to think and reflect. The goal of critical thinking is for students to be able to think deeply and make good decisions so that they can live their lives better. The conventional way of teaching must be changed, and you should become a facilitator in your classroom instead of a lecturer. As your students develop a critical thinking mindset, you will soon find yourself in a position where your role as teacher seems to be different.

(305 words)

1. *According to the author, are critical thinking skills important for young children?* （根拠　　行目）
    a. It's very important.　　b. It's not important.　　c. It's optional.
2. *According to the author, is it difficult to practice questions for critical thinking in English?* （根拠　　行目）
    a. Yes, it is.　　b. No, it isn't.　　c. No, it doesn't.
3. *What kind of teacher does the author think is best?* （根拠　　行目）
    a. A good and traditional teacher　　b. A facilitator　　c. A computer programmer

---

知っておこう！キーワード | *Choose the correct answer.* 次の語の意味をa〜eの中から選びましょう。

1. recognize (　　)　　2. mindset (　　)　　3. conventional (　　)
4. critical thinking (　　)　　5. facilitator (　　)
a. クリティカル・シンキング，批判的思考　　b. ものの見方，心の有り様　　c. 認識する
d. ファシリテーター，進行役，まとめ役　　e. 従来の

Part 3

> **EXERCISES** 確認問題
> 1. Complete the sentences according to the directions. 指示に従って文を完成しましょう。
> 2. After checking your answers, practice reading the correct sentences aloud.
>   答え合わせをしたら，正しい文を音読しましょう。

❶ *Make English sentences using the words below.* T60
日本文を読み，英語の語句を並びかえてください。（文頭は大文字ではありません）

1. それはどんな動画ですか？
   (is / video / what / of / kind / it)?
   _____

2. それは世界の夏休みについてです。
   (world / about / the / it / summer / is / in / vacations).
   _____

3. 聞こえたものを私に言ってください。
   (what / me / you / tell / heard).
   _____

4. 何が異なっているのか見てみましょう。
   (is / what / let's / see / different).
   _____

5. 子ども達は情報のオーバーロード（過負荷）の驚異にさらされています。
   (There is one word missing. 1語を補ってください。)
   (threat / are / children / information / of / the / overload).
   _____

❷ *Translate the Japanese sentences into English.* T61
日本文を読み，本文を参考にして英文を書いてください。

1. よく見て，見たものを私に言ってください。
   Watch and _____

2. "table" はなんだか知っていますか？（Use "know."）
   _____

3. 動画を見て他に気がつきましたか？（Use "anything else."）
   _____

4. オーストラリアでは夏休みが12月に6週間あります。
   They have _____

5. あなたは教室では講師ではなくファシリテーターになるべきです。（Use "instead of."）
   _____

Developing Children's Thinking Skills (1)

Lesson 13

Developing Children's Thinking Skills (2)

考えさせる指導法（2）— より豊かな思考力を目指して

　前のレッスンでは，リスニングや動画教材などを通じて，内容理解をした後の活動が大切だと述べました。各種教材や教科書にも，児童の思考力を育む様々な活動が用意されています。さらに，授業を発展させるにはどのような授業作りができるでしょうか。

活動	内容	例
調べ学習	学習内容に関連する情報や映像を探し，発表する方法。Show and Tell 形式での発表は積極性を促す。	（国際的関心）外国の夏休みについて （環境）地域のリサイクルについて （趣味や興味から）世界大会の結果や様子
ゲームや クイズ形式	学習内容に関連するゲームやクイズをする方法。動画や画像を見て，教師からのクイズを考えたり，自分で調べたことをクイズにすることでその過程で気づきが出てくる。 また，ディスカッションへのウォーミングアップとしても活用可能。例えば，教師は，3択のクイズを用意して回答させる際，聞き取りの練習問題に続いて，「なぜ」「どうして」と考えさせる設問を入れることで選択肢をヒントに意見を引き出すことができる。	登場人物3人が，それぞれ夏休みにしたこと，その感想を話している映像資料を視聴させた後，名前，行った場所，したことなどのクイズを出す。発展として，英語で過去形の練習も兼ね，聞き取った内容や自分の夏休みについて発表させる。
教科横断型学習	社会科や理科における，国や地域，環境問題，生態系などの内容に関連した学習方法。 英語の授業でも What's this? や Do you like ...? などの表現を使って，英語の語彙や表現を使いながら気づきを促す。	他教科で，各国の祭りなどの文化の特徴について比較させたり，地域の気候の違いについて調べ学習につなげたりする。
内容言語統合型学習 CLIL（クリル：Content and Language Integrated Learning）	理科や社会などの教科学習と語学学習を統合した方法。教科内容を題材に様々な言語活動を行うことで，英語の4技能を高めることができるとされている。CLILは，欧州でも活用されており，日本でも子ども達の発信能力を高め，英語教育の質的向上をもたらすものと期待され，理科，社会，算数などを英語で教える試みがなされている。児童の認知発達段階に応じた多様な学習を行うことが可能であり，既存の知識を使って考えるだけでなく，批判的に考えるといった作業をするため，深い思考力を伴う学習方法である。	社会科：産地，地球環境，国・都市の名称，国旗，特産品 理科：生物の名称，色，食性，生息地，太陽系 国語：既習の物語と同様または類似の英語の物語（かぐや姫とおやゆび姫など） 算数：数字，四則演算，図形，グラフ 技術家庭：料理の仕方，材料の名前 音楽：英語の歌 体育：動作，ダンスなど 図工：色，形，その他図画工作を用いた様々なアクティビティなど

　こういった様々な活動をする際に，英語のみで行うかどうかが議論されています。児童が調べた内容をクイズにして，What's this? などの英語だけで授業を行ったり，簡単な発表の雛形を与えて英語で発表させたりすることも可能でしょう。また，論理的思考やクリティカル・シンキングなどの深い思考力を養うには，母語の使用も有効です。英語で得た情報をもとに，自分の言葉で論理的思考や成否を吟味し検証し，生きる力につなげていく授業作りにも発展させることができます。もちろん，児童の関心が高ければ英語で意見を発言させても良いと思いますが，英語の語彙が限られているため，英語の授業中は英語，連携した他教科の授業の中では，日本語で発言させる，または同じ英語の授業中でも日本語を使ってもよい「学びの時間」をとるなど，「場」の区別をしっかりつけると，言語の混乱を防ぐことができます。英語の授業における活動では，児童が高揚した気持ちであることも多いため，明確な区別をすることが大切です。

Part 3

四則演算（the four operations）や太陽系（the solar system）など既習のものでも，英語で学ぶことで世界観が広がります。得意科目や既知の内容を学ぶことで，英語への関心をさらに引き出すことも期待できます。

Let's Talk

ALT: How about teaching the students math in English?
HRT: That's a great idea! They just learned numbers last week. How do you say 1+1=2 (ichi-tasu-ichi-wa-ni) in English? One plus one equals two, is that correct?
ALT: It is correct, but we say "One plus one is two," especially in elementary school.
HRT: Oh, really? Let them try plus, minus, ah … .
ALT: Addition, subtraction, multiplication, and division, or the four operations.
HRT: I wonder if the students can remember them?
ALT: Oh, they can say, plus, minus, times, and divided.

Conversation

Listen to the dialogue and fill in the blanks, then role play the conversation.
会話文を聞いて，空欄に適語を入れなさい。その後，パートナーと会話をしましょう。

ALT: I have 1._____ eggs in my hand.

HRT: I have four eggs in my hand.

ALT: How 2._____ eggs do we have in our hands?

S1: Seven!

ALT: Yes! That's 3._____! Seven eggs. Repeat after me. Three 4._____ four is seven.

Ss: Three 4._____ four is seven.

ALT: Good! Now, listen … "Four plus nine is … ?"

S2: 5._____!

ALT: 5._____ or thirteen?

S2: Ah! Thirteen! Thirteen!

ALT: You did 6._____!

〈HRT: writing on the blackboard or showing on the screen〉

ALT: Five plus six is eleven, nine 7._____ six is three, three 8._____ four is twelve, fifteen divided 9._____ five is three.

──〈After practicing〉──

ALT: Let's try a 10._____! Do we have any volunteers?

Developing Children's Thinking Skills (2) **63**

Let's Read

Read the passage and answer the questions.
文を読んで次の質問に答えましょう。答えの根拠となる文の行数を（　）に書きましょう。

Good afternoon. I'm Haruto Tanaka, a teacher of the third graders at Nansei Elementary School. Today, I would like to share my experience when I taught a lesson on creative thinking.

First, I followed the step in the textbook showing a video of three children from different countries who were talking about their summer vacation. Let me play it for a minute.

As you saw, it was not hard for students to understand what the children in the video did during the summer with simple English and the aid of visual information. The stories were fascinating especially because my students just came back from summer vacation. I played it several times so that they could fill in the provided comparison table. They were good at using the past tense when they talked about the vacations in the video. They practiced more past tense by telling memories from their summer vacations. I asked them if they noticed anything from the table, but I could not get many responses as they had limited vocabulary.

Next day, I put the comparison table on the blackboard and showed the video again in the social studies lesson. Then I asked them the same question but in Japanese. They were far more active describing it than they were in English. They said, "I want a summer vacation that long!," "Interesting! Summer holiday in the cold season?," "Which is correct, summer vacation or summer holiday?," "I want to go to summer camp in America!," "Do you know there's no summer vacation in Singapore?," and so on. I was quite happy to hear their various questions and opinions, which I believe stimulated their intellectual curiosity.

Thank you for listening to my presentation. I'd be happy to address any comments or questions.

(293 words)

1. *What is the theme of the presentation?*（根拠＿＿行目）
    a. Summer vacation
    b. Teaching how to make a comparison table
    c. How to make an English lesson for creative thinking
2. *What kind of video did he show at the presentation?*（根拠＿＿行目）
    a. How children learned the past tense
    b. About summer vacations in the world
    c. How to create a table
3. *Did he have a lesson in English or Japanese?*（根拠＿＿行目）
    a. He used English only.
    b. He used Japanese and English in the English lesson.
    c. He used both English in the English lesson, and Japanese in the social studies lesson.

Part 3

EXERCISES 確認問題

1. **Complete the sentences according to the directions.** 指示に従って文を完成しましょう。
2. **After checking your answers, practice reading the correct sentences aloud.**
   答え合わせをしたら，正しい文を音読しましょう。

❶ *Make English sentences using the words below.* T65
日本文を読み，英語の語句を並びかえてください。（文頭は大文字ではありません）

1. これは正解ですか？
   (correct / is / this)?

   _____

2. それはいい案ですね。
   (that's / idea / great / a)!

   _____

3. それらは，加減乗除，または四則演算です。
   They are (subtraction, / operations / and / division / , / or / the / four / addition, / multiplication).

   _____

4. 先週，彼らはちょうど数字を学んだばかりです。(There is one word missing. 1語を補ってください。)
   (numbers / learned / just / last / they).

   _____

5. 動画の中の子ども達が夏休み中に何をしたのかを理解するのは難しくありませんでした。
   It was not hard (what / the / for / to / children / the / understand / students / did / video / in) during the summer.

   _____

❷ *Translate the Japanese sentences into English.* T66
日本文を読み，本文を参考にして英文を書いてください。

1. 私達は手に卵をいくつ持っているでしょう？
   How _____

2. 15 ÷ 5 = 3 (Spell out all the numbers and use "is." 数字を英語で書きましょう。)

   _____

3. 児童に算数を英語で教えるのはいかがでしょう？(Use "how.")

   _____

4. 誰か有志の（やってくれる）人？
   Do we _____

5. その様々な質問を聞いて，私は大変満足でした。(Use "quite happy.")

   _____

Developing Children's Thinking Skills (2)

Part 4 評価と模擬授業

Lesson 14

Evaluation

> 評価を考える — CAN-DO リストの活用

　評価とは，児童が学習においてどのような力をつけたか，その成果を具体的に捉えるものです。評価を通じて教師の指導法が適正であったかどうかを振り返り，指導の充実を図る改善の機会ともなります。評価を受けた児童にとっては，自らの学習態度や学習方法を振り返り，学習面で足りないところを補い，また教師の助言を参考にし，軌道修正を行い，その後の学習面の改善が促される契機になります。保護者においても，家庭における児童の学習を鑑みる機会を与えられます。また教師も児童を評価することで，自分の指導を振り返ることができますので，指導と評価の一体につながります。学習指導と評価は一体化されるべきであり，指導計画を作成し（Plan），それを授業で実践し（Do），その成果を振り返り評価として表し（Check），指導の改善を図る（Act）という一連の流れ（PDCAサイクル）で捉えることができます。

　「小学校外国語活動・外国語研修ガイドブック」（文部科学省）には，「指導と評価の一体化を図る中で，論述やレポート作成，発表，グループでの話し合い，作品の制作等といった多様な活動に取り組ませるパフォーマンス評価などを取り入れ，ペーパーテストの結果にとどまらない，多面的・多角的な評価を行っていくことが必要」とされています。教師は指導の段階から発表やグループ活動など，様々な学習方法を取り入れるようにしましょう。

　コミュニケーションという計量化しにくいものを評価するのは難しい課題といえます。欧州では外国語学習者の熟達度・習得状況を測るために，「ヨーロッパ言語共通参照枠，CEFR（セファール：Common European Framework of Reference for Language）」と呼ばれる国際標準規格を設定し，利用しています。日本でも文部科学省がこの枠組みを参考にした英語力の学習到達目標をCAN-DOリストとしてまとめました。このリストは，「学習者が英語で〜することができる」と到達目標を具体的に設定したものです。ペーパーテストの結果や教科書内容だけにとどまらない様々な学習活動を評価するため，教師は長期的かつ中期的な到達目標を設定する必要があります。つまり，卒業する時や学年の終わりに何ができるようになっているかを目標として考えるのです。また，このリストを学習者に提示することで，道標を示す手助けとなり，学習効果が上がることが期待されます。CAN-DOリストは中・高等学校の外国語を対象としています。各自治体，各学校で小学校外国語活動・外国語におけるCAN-DOリストの作成が求められた場合，児童の実態や地域の特徴を把握した上で作成，活用することが重要です。

Part 4

> 教師が英語で質問したことに対し，児童が日本語で返事をするやり取りは教室でよく見られます。
> 強制的に英語を話させるのではなく，英語を話そうとする前向きな姿勢を育てることが大切です。

Let's Talk

ALT: Do you have any plans during the spring vacation?
S: Plan? Vacation?
ALT: Yes. You use the word *plan* in Japanese. And you have three long vacations every year, a summer vacation, a winter vacation, and a spring vacation.
S: わかった，春休みのこと。
ALT: Yes, you can listen to me and understand what I said. Great work!
S: Thank you.

Conversation

Listen to the dialogue and fill in the blanks, then role play the conversation.
会話文を聞いて，空欄に適語を入れなさい。その後，パートナーと会話をしましょう。

ALT: Do we need 1._____ evaluate our fifth- and sixth-grade students' English?

HRT: Yes, that's right. Evaluation is very difficult in any 2._____.

ALT: Yes, we have to evaluate not 3._____ the results of the written tests, but also the students' speaking abilities. I think it's especially hard 4._____ Japanese teachers to judge their speaking abilities.

HRT: And we have to consider their 5._____ or motivation to communicate in English. Actually, the students are evaluated based on 6._____ criteria.

ALT: OK. But how do you evaluate them?

HRT: At the 7._____ of the class, children write their 8._____, which tell us what they learned or how 9._____ they understand. We can partly assess them from their comments. We also assess them from their performance in presentations.

ALT: OK. It 10._____ like a lot of work to do assessments.

※ Criteria とは3つの観点を指し，それらは①知識・技能，②思考・判断・表現，③主体的に学習に取り組む態度です。

Evaluation

Let's Read

Read the passage and answer the questions.
文を読んで次の質問に答えましょう。答えの根拠となる文の行数を（　）に書きましょう。

English education is starting at an earlier age in Japan. Students in upper grades of elementary schools are evaluated according to guidelines set by the government. To create these guidelines, the Ministry of Education, Culture, Sports, Science and Technology (MEXT) referenced the European CEFR framework.

The guidelines contain a list of aims that are meant to motivate students to achieve a certain level of English. For example, a sixth-grade student is expected to be able to answer basic questions about their daily life. But this list of goals shouldn't be applied to students of all levels or in all regions of the country. One approach to evaluate students is for schools and local governments to create their own list, called a CAN-DO list, based on the guidelines to fit the requirements of their schools and students.

There are many things that educators should consider when creating a CAN-DO list. For example, they must make sure that it matches the philosophy of their school. Another thing to consider is the students' motivation. One problem with writing a list of goals is that children can lose their motivation to study English if the goals aren't achievable.

The guidelines also aim to prepare students for English classes in junior high schools. Most students will go to a junior high school in the local area, so it's good to have an understanding of the English curriculum at local schools.

Although English is a new subject at Japanese elementary schools, the government has created guidelines based on the experiences of other countries. But educators at each school must decide how to apply this in their classroom so that they can best prepare their students for not only junior high school, but a world where English is growing more important.

(294 words)

1. *What did MEXT reference to create the guidelines?* （根拠＿＿行目）
   a. A CAN-DO list
   b. The European CEFR framework
   c. The English curriculum of local schools
2. *What approach should schools and local governments use to evaluate students under the guidelines?* （根拠＿＿行目）
   a. The European CEFR framework
   b. The guidelines that MEXT has written
   c. A CAN-DO list that they create based on the guidelines
3. *Which of the following is a problem with CAN-DO lists?* （根拠＿＿行目）
   a. If the aims are not achievable, it could lead to students losing motivation to study.
   b. There are not enough teachers who can write CAN-DO lists.
   c. The CAN-DO lists must be the same as those at junior high schools.

知っておこう！キーワード | *Choose the correct answer.* 次の語の意味をa〜eの中から選びましょう。

1. aim (　)　2. evaluate (　)　3. achieve (　)　4. educator (　)
5. consider (　)
a. 教育者　b. 熟考する　c. ねらい　d. 達成する　e. 評価する

Part 4

EXERCISES 確認問題
1. *Complete the sentences according to the directions.* 指示に従って文を完成しましょう。
2. *After checking your answers, practice reading the correct sentences aloud.*
   答え合わせをしたら、正しい文を音読しましょう。

❶ *Make English sentences using the words below.* T70
   日本文を読み，英語の語句を並びかえてください。（文頭は大文字ではありません）

   1. 私たちは児童たちの英語の成績をつける必要がありますか？
      (evaluate / we / need / do / the / to / English / students')?

      _____

   2. 休みの間，何か計画はありますか？
      (the / during / you / vacation / do / any / have / plans)?

      _____

   3. どの教科でも評価はとても難しいのです。
      (evaluation / difficult / subject / in / any / very / is).

      _____

   4. 私たちは発表の出来ばえからも児童を評価します。
      (from / we / assess / their / presentations / performance / in / students / also / the).

      _____

   5. ほとんどの児童たちは地元の中学校に通うでしょう。
      （There is one word missing. 1語を補ってください。）

      (go / will / most / a / to / area / students / junior high school / in / the).

      _____

❷ *Translate the Japanese sentences into English.* T71
   日本文を読み，本文を参考にして英文を書いてください。

   1. 毎年３つの長い休みがありますね。

      You have _____

   2. 子ども達が英語を学ぶ意欲を失う可能性があります。

      Children can _____

   3. 評価をするのは大変な仕事のようですね。(Use "assessments" and "sounds.")

      _____

   4. 児童は３つの観点で評価されます。(Use "evaluated" and "based.")

      _____

   5. 日本人の教師にとって，児童たちのスピーキング能力を判断するのは難しいです。
      (Use "judge" and "abilities.")

      _____

Lesson 15

Teaching Practice

模擬授業 ― 指導案作成から授業実践まで

　学習指導案は，教員が授業を進めるための計画書であり，授業の設計図，航海図，シナリオともいわれます。授業そのものの質を高め，授業の方向を確かなものとするために書かれます。子ども達を主人公にするために，子ども達自身とその置かれている学習環境を理解し，子ども達に届く教育実践を考えて作成します。教師が何を教えるかではなく，子ども達は何を学ぶかという視点を意識するようにしましょう。

　具体的には，単元の目標，教材に対する考え方，本時の授業のねらい，実際の授業の展開案，どのように評価するかを記載します。指導案には，研究授業や公開授業のときなどに示す詳細なもの（細案）から，授業の流れを示した略式のもの（略案）があります。文部科学省や教育委員会のウェブサイトには小学校英語のテキストを使った指導案の例が豊富に用意されています。調査し実際にどのような授業になるのか考え，それぞれの指導案の良い点，改善点について話し合ってみましょう。

　指導案を作成する際は，調査した指導案を参考にしましょう。十分に推敲したら，ペアまたはグループ内でティーム・ティーチングの役割を決め，何度も音読をします。さらに，他のチームと組んで互いに児童役をするのが良いでしょう。

　指導案は，以下のような視点で推敲し，模擬授業の際にも，各項目ごとに客観的評価をしましょう。

声・話し方	・話し方は，明瞭で，正確かつ的確か。 ・声量，速さは適切でわかりやすいか。
表情・アイコンタクト	・表情が豊かでメリハリがあるか。 ・単語や文の意味により表現を変えているか。 ・常にアイコンタクトがあり，児童一人一人，クラス全体を見ているか。 ・指導案を見ることは全くないか，最小限であるか。
ティーチャー・トーク	・児童のレベルに合った語彙で，非常にわかりやすく，簡単でかつ明瞭な言葉で話しているか。 ・長すぎず，短すぎず，適度な長さの文や言葉であるか。
英語	・英文法に誤りがないか。 ・発音，イントネーションは正確か。
適切な指示	・指示に無駄がなくわかりやすいか。 ・活動の順番や動線を考えて，用意周到な指示がなされているか。 ・英語がメインだが，場面に応じ効果的に日本語を使用しているか。
授業構成・時間配分	・Warming Up（挨拶，導入，復習など），Main，Consolidation の３区分が明確にあり，かつ繋がりのある構成であるか。 ・児童の学習状況に合わせた時間配分であるか。

Part 4

Model Reading in the Lesson Plan
Listen to the model reading in the lesson plan and fill in the blanks.
以下の指導案の空欄を埋めましょう。

T72
S44

本時の目標：前時までに児童は基本的な挨拶と歌，感情表現の英語を学んでいる。本時では，感情表現に合うジェスチャーをしながら，次時の自発的な生徒同士の会話につなげる。

扱う表現：How are you feeling today? I'm … fine/sleepy/hungry/tired/sad/great/so-so/hot/cold など感情や状態を表す言葉。

過程	児童の活動	教師の活動	指導上の留意点
挨拶 （5分）	Good afternoon. I'm fine. I'm hungry. 教師の挨拶に対して，各自の今の気持ちを表現する。 元気よく Hello! などと挨拶するだけでもよい。 The "Hello song." ♪Hello, hello, hello, how are you?	(1) Good _____! How are you today? 元気よく挨拶をして明るい雰囲気で授業がスタートする。それぞれの児童の表現を拾って，Are you OK? などの声掛けをする。 (2) Let's sing a song _____	その日の天候などに応じて，「暑い」など，様々な表現やジェスチャーをつけながら，わかりやすく導入していく。 発声練習，発音練習も兼ねて楽しく行う。
導入 （10分）	I'm hungry! I'm sleepy! Yes!	Let's Speak Together 1 (p.8) の感情表現の復習。 (3) How are you _____ today? (4) Great! Now let's _____ a video!	お腹空いた，眠いなどの体感を英語で表す復習をする。動画を見せ，発音や表現の復習をしながら英語表現とジェスチャーのつながりに気づかせる。
アクティビティ （25分）	児童も言いながらジェスチャーを真似する。 (8) Good. I don't know. Me? Good _____! Come here! Give me _____!	(5) Now, _____ the textbook _____ page eight. (6) Repeat after me and do _____ I do. (7) _____ let's try! (8) Good. I don't know. Me? Good _____! Come here! Give me _____!	テキストで，気づきを確かめ知識として理解させてから，言いながらジェスチャーすることを真似させる。 言いながらジェスチャーをする。正確性よりも，ジェスチャーを通じて，英語が伝達の手段であること，日本語のジェスチャーとは違うことなどを楽しんでもらう。
まとめ （5分）	自己評価をする（「振り返りカード」の記入）。	Let's sing the "Good-bye song" together! 振り返りカードを配る。 Take one and pass them around.	振り返りさせることで，学習項目の認知的効果を実感させる。

Teaching Practice 73

Let's Read

Read the passage and answer the questions.
文を読んで次の質問に答えましょう。答えの根拠となる文の行数を（　）に書きましょう。

　A teaching practicum is a required course to obtain a teaching certificate for elementary school. It is usually taken in your junior or senior year for a few weeks. It aims to give student teachers an opportunity to practice what they have learned. While it is fun to take over a class and teach children, there are a number of things you should prepare for and put into effect in the class. 5

　Looking back on my time, there were some things I was glad I did. However, there were also other things I wish I had done differently. To be successful in the teaching practicum program, you have to work hard, be organized, and be up for anything. There is a lot of work involved. The teacher is not always next to you for every step of the way. They are observers and supervisors. You can ask questions, but ultimately it is up to you to 10 make decisions and get things finished without precise instructions. Remember to pay attention to what you have learned and stay dedicated to the work that is put in front of you.

　One of the things I should have done was networking with other student teachers. First, I did not seek advice from senior students who had done it before. I could have referred to the lesson plans that previous student teachers had left for us, but I ignored 15 them. I thought I learned and knew everything, and that I could create my original lesson plans with new activities. Next, I was too busy to talk with other student teachers. I went to school early every day and stayed late to prepare for the classes, but I thought it was a waste of time chatting with other student teachers. Talking with colleagues would have given me practical information, inspiration, lesson ideas, and more. (308 words) 20

1. *According to the passage, what is the objective of a teaching practicum?* （根拠___行目）
    a. Giving children an opportunity to learn English
    b. Providing student teachers with an opportunity to practice teaching
    c. Giving teachers an opportunity to teach children
2. *Which is NOT correct about what you have to do as a student teacher?* （根拠___行目）
    a. Working hard
    b. Making decisions
    c. Participating in other subject classes
3. *What did the author do during her teaching practicum period?* （根拠___行目）
    a. She got advice from her senior friend.
    b. She talked with teachers too much.
    c. She created a new lesson plan.

知っておこう！キーワード | *Choose the correct answer.* 次の語の意味を a～e の中から選びましょう。

1. up to you (　　)　　2. student teacher (　　)　　3. senior year (　　)
4. teaching practicum (　　)　　5. for reference (　　)

a. 教育実習　　b. 教育実習生　　c. アメリカの大学の最終学年　　d. あなた次第　　e. 参考のために

Part 4

> **EXERCISES** 確認問題
> *Create a lesson plan based on what you have learned.*
> これまで学習したことや，調べたことを参考に模擬授業に使用する授業案を作成しましょう。

本時の目標：＿＿＿＿＿＿＿＿＿＿＿＿＿＿＿＿＿＿＿＿＿＿＿＿＿＿＿＿

扱う表現：＿＿＿＿＿＿＿＿＿＿＿＿＿＿＿＿＿＿＿＿＿＿＿＿＿＿＿＿＿

過程	児童の活動	教師の活動	指導上の留意点
挨拶（5分）			
導入（10分）			
アクティビティ（25分）			
まとめ（5分）			

Teaching Practice

| 著作権法上，無断複写・複製は禁じられています。 |

Let's Have Fun Teaching English   [B-893]
  —From Theory to Practice

ここから始めよう児童英語！ —理論から実践へ—

| 第1刷 | 2019年4月1日 |
| 第6刷 | 2024年4月10日 |

著 者	小原弥生	Yayoi Obara
	豊田典子	Noriko Toyoda
	髙橋まり	Mari Takahashi
	スティーヴン・ロジャース	Steven Rogers

発行者　南雲一範　Kazunori Nagumo
発行所　株式会社　南雲堂
　　　　〒162-0801　東京都新宿区山吹町361
　　　　NAN'UN-DO Publishing Co., Ltd.
　　　　361 Yamabuki-cho, Shinjuku-ku, Tokyo 162-0801, Japan
　　　　振替口座：00160-0-46863
　　　　TEL: 03-3268-2311（営業部：学校関係）
　　　　　　　03-3268-2384（営業部：書店関係）
　　　　　　　03-3268-2387（編集部）
　　　　FAX: 03-3269-2486

編集者　丸小雅臣／伊藤宏実
組版・印刷　啓文堂
装　丁　NONdesign
検　印　省　略
コード　ISBN978-4-523-17893-4 C0082

Printed in Japan

落丁・乱丁，その他不良品がございましたら，お取り替えいたします。

E-mail　nanundo@post.email.ne.jp
URL　https://www.nanun-do.co.jp/